Jesus, His Word and Work

D0108064

GOD'S WORD TODAY V

A New Study Guide to the Bible

James M. Reese O.S.F.S.

Jesus, His Word and Work

The Gospels of Matthew, Mark and Luke

Suggestions for Reflection
by Sr. Jeanne Monahan O.P.

PUEBLO PUBLISHING COMPANY

NEW YORK

Imprimi potest: *J. Stuart Dooling, O.S.F.S.*
                   Provincial, Oblates of St. Francis de Sales
                   August 6, 1978

Nihil Obstat: *Daniel V. Flynn, J.C.D.*
                   Censor Librorum

Imprimatur: *Joseph T. O'Keefe*
                   Vicar General
                   Archdiocese of New York
                   August 8, 1978

Design: Frank Kacmarcik, D.F.A.

ISBN: 0-916134-32-6

Printed in the United States of America

CONTENTS

PREFACE

Interest in the Scriptures continues to grow. Men and women individually and in groups read, reflect on, discuss, pray from the Bible. I have taught, led, participated in such groups. This participation has convinced me that, despite all the worthwhile material on the Bible already available, there are still gaps to be filled for those people who truly care about the Bible but have had little or no preparation to extract its riches.

Several excellent guides to the Bible exist in the format of booklet series in which each volume provides commentary and explanation on a separate book of the Bible. However, for someone becoming acquainted with the Bible, to work through each book one by one can be a formidable task.

Other books focus on themes and main ideas distilled from the whole Bible. As valuable as such theologies and over-all views are, there is still a need for a familiarity with the *text* of the Bible itself.

In this series, substantial portions of the Scriptures—extensive enough to convey style, language, tone—are the indispensable starting point. Essential background and explanation are provided and the lasting import of the text is suggested. Possibilities for individual or group reflection are offered.

When the reader has completed this series, he will have encountered many themes and main ideas, and this through a selected and guided reading of the text itself. This over-all view can be filled in by further study of the individual books of the Bible.

The general plan emerges from a listing of the titles in this series. It is my strong recommendation that anyone using the series begin with Volume I. If the principles presented there are grasped, the spadework will be done for understanding what follows.

"Indeed, God's word is living and effective, sharper than any two-edged sword. It penetrates and divides soul and spirit, joints and marrow; it judges the reflections and thoughts of the heart" (Hebrews 4.12).

Emil A. Wcela
Series Editor

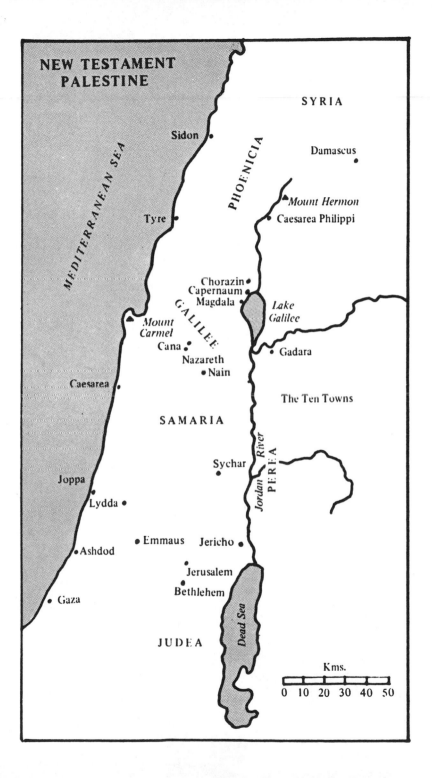

CHAPTER I

INTRODUCING THE SYNOPTIC GOSPELS

If Jesus lived in this century, his death would have received media coverage. The event would be preserved in film and on sound track.

But would we have better insight into the meaning of that event? For believers the answer is no. The Gospels show the Church of every age and nation that Jesus wrought the most profound change in human history.

We moderns—products of a scientific society—find it hard to relate to the Gospels except in terms of historical records. But they are more than that; they are primarily *revelations*. That means they open up to us the reality of Jesus as God's Son.

Jesus was a religious person. His whole life was God-ward bound. The language of the Gospels is religious. They demand the whole life of believers.

WHY SO LONG DELAYED?

Before the Gospels could be written, the experience of Jesus had to be interiorized by his followers. The first step in sharing any spiritual value is to enjoy inner communion with its reality. The closest followers of Jesus did not arrive at this intense involvement during his earthly life. Throughout that time they were frequently self-centered and ambitious.

Only after the risen Jesus had sent his Holy Spirit upon them did his apostles have religious insight to grasp what he did and said and was. They began to share these insights. This apostolic witness attracted converts and led to the formation of believing communities.

Only as new converts, who did not know Jesus directly, joined their ranks was writing needed. Before that time members of the various communities shared their faith by word of mouth.

The actual process of composing the Gospels was the final stage of a long procedure. This introductory chapter will build on and fill in the brief section on the Gospels in the opening volume of this series (Emil A. Wcela, *The Bible*, pp. 73-76) and trace the major steps leading to the formation of three of the four New Testament Gospels, Matthew, Mark and Luke (abbreviated Mt, Mk, Lk). These are called "synoptic Gospels" because they exhibit the same basic structure. If they are printed in parallel columns, their interrelation can be seen "at a glance." The Greek term for this phrase is *synopsis*. So the adjective *synoptic* is used as a technical word to describe these three Gospels.

NOT THE FIRST NEW TESTAMENT WRITINGS

Before it was necessary or even possible to compose Gospels as we know them, the Christian community had to grow and face changes. It had to face up to an uncertain future in a hostile world. The Christians could not sit back and wait idly for the glorious kingdom Jesus preached. That stage was in God's hands. Their task was to become a Church—a praying assembly of believers.

Members of these local groups of worshipers were destined to suffer in their efforts to follow Jesus. Human knowledge begins with concrete experience. Only those who have suffered for Jesus know him and the power of his resurrection.

The spread of these local churches is described in schematic form in the Acts of the Apostles. That book shows how the Church's center of gravity gradually shifted from Jewish Christians to converts from paganism.

The apostle Paul was responsible in great part for this change. The impetus of his encounter with the risen Jesus led him to preach complete equality within the Church for all. In his missionary travels Paul began his preaching in Jewish synagogues. His success in attracting believers in the Lord Jesus stirred up violent opposition.

Again and again Paul was driven out of cities. He had to leave his task of forming local communities incomplete. This is the circumstance that started the collection of writings that eventually grew into the New Testament. He wrote letters to answer problems that arose on a local level.

Paul's letters scarcely mention the earthly life of Jesus. He never had any need to deal with it. The Holy Spirit of the risen Jesus kept manifesting himself so vehemently that early believers seldom looked back into the events of Jesus' life on earth. Paul put his emphasis on the death and resurrection of Christ as the heart of God's saving work. But gradually second generation Christians felt a need to know more about the early Jesus and began to seek information.

RAPID EXPANSION OF COMMUNITIES

The rapid increase in number and size of local churches brought about a crisis in how to keep the faith vibrant. Most people cannot sustain a high level of enthusiasm over long periods of time.

When believers went to other parts of the Roman Empire, they formed new churches in remote places. These groups came together regularly to do what Jesus had commanded the night before he died. By the eucharistic meal, they celebrated his death and resurrection and their hope in his coming again.

The full meaning of the death of Jesus demanded that Christians know what led to his being rejected by his own. So it was important for believers to know the words and deeds of Jesus. Only his powerful example and the impulse of the Spirit could produce in them mutual love strong enough to risk all for the kingdom of God.

Such Christian love was the fruit of a faith that held out the sure hope of eternal life with Jesus. This hope appealed strongly to the poor and exploited of the Roman Empire. So the unity existing within local Christian communities acted like a magnet to draw new converts. But this rapid increase in membership also created new challenges.

New converts had to grow in knowledge about Jesus and the moral demands of his teaching. No well-established central authority existed to insure uniform belief and lifestyle. Of course communication was slow and irregular.

As more and more original eyewitnesses died or were martyred, remaining apostolic leaders faced the problem of providing reliable grounds for future believers. Questions from new members required that preachers present short narratives about what Jesus said and did. The answers were never uninvolved, impersonal accounts.

EXPERIENCE OF PRIMARY WITNESSES

Of all the eyewitnesses and companions of the earthly Jesus, the apostles played the most important role in the early Church. After receiving the Holy Spirit they began to proclaim that the Father had raised Jesus from among the dead.

The apostles did not treat the life, death and resurrection of Jesus as past events, but as a present and ongoing dynamism in the Church. They proclaimed and preached the good news. The "proclamation" and "preaching" are important. They became technical words for two stages in the conversion process. To *proclaim* is to present Jesus as saving Lord and to appeal for conversion. To *preach* is to offer a developed program for personalizing Gospel values.

These early preachers were skillful in adapting the good news to the changing needs of their audiences. The great variety of approaches in portraying Jesus helps us see why he did not write any literature himself.

As incarnate son of David, Jesus was linked to a particular moment in history with its cultural limitations. Yet his coming was for all mankind. In refusing to write himself, Jesus cut the good news free from the cultural moorings of one particular culture.

GOSPEL AS UNIVERSAL REVELATION

The Gospel is revelation. It is expressed in unique religious language. It is God-ward language, not language about God. The dynamism of the Gospel sweeps those who proclaim it along on its path to God.

Religious language offers a challenge to those who speak it as well as to those who hear it. They must make a choice—for God or against him. So the Gospels had to be written by those who had made a choice for Jesus. Their aim was to share this good news with others. But first they had to clothe their convictions with the flesh of their personal experience.

As they went about forming new communities, Christian preachers gradually developed various phraseologies and key words that epitomized the message and were easy for people to memorize. Historical biblical criticism has studied the apostolic preaching and developed certain technical methods to identify its various elements. These methods are:

Tradition criticism—an investigation of the oral materials underlying the written Gospels.

Form criticism—a study of the origin and growth of the individual units of oral tradition that have contributed to the development of the canonical Gospels.

Redaction criticism—a method isolating and identifying the personal theological contributions of each Gospel author.

Today, fortunately, lay men and women can find the fruits of these specialized studies in contemporary commentaries and introductions to the New Testament. Most believers are primarily interested in the Gospels. Before treating each of the synoptic Gospels individually, it is important to become acquainted with some basic elements common to all three of them.

My approach is to begin with small units of oral or written tradition because the Gospels are built around them. Once a reader becomes acquainted with these, it is easier to move to an overall view of each Gospel. Our first clue to the importance of this oral or written tradition that underlies all three Gospels is found in Luke.

GROWTH OF SMALL GOSPEL UNITS

Please read: Luke 1.1-4

The evangelist Luke opens his Gospel with a short, artistic preface or prologue. He directs it to "dearest Theophilus" meaning "friend of God." It is not certain whether Theophilus is a real person. He could be simply the model disciple. In either case, Luke would then be giving his Gospel a personal thrust.

Or, Theophilus could be the patron who paid to have the Gospel written. At the time of Luke each copy of a book had to be written out in longhand. It was a process requiring a good deal of time and money. Luke may have searched for a rich person to pay the bill and have dedicated his Gospel to him.

The rest of Luke's prologue tells why he wrote. He was dissatisfied with accounts about the activity of Jesus that were circulating in his community. These accounts were evidently disconnected and failed to communicate a profound insight into the Christ event. Not an eyewitness himself, Luke sought out the reliable ones. By relying on them, he can now offer a comprehensive view of Christ in a way to inspire confidence in his readers about their faith.

The mention of previous writings in this prologue points to a great deal of literary activity in early Christian communities. A careful reading of the synoptic Gospels indicates that the evangelists incorporated many earlier written units into their Gospels.

Each evangelist modified this traditional material according to his own needs. This could be done by removing or adding details, by combining scenes or transferring material from one place to another in the account. I will give some examples in later chapters.

Luke modifies the material he uses as much as Matthew and Mark. Why then does he call his account "orderly"? The answer is that he is not talking about chronological order. He is working with a deeper principle of unity. Gospels are theological writings. They reveal the work of Jesus as saving.

LOSS OF THE EARLIER ACCOUNTS

The success of Luke's Gospel—as well as those of Matthew and Mark—effectively destroyed the earlier accounts he mentions. These small writings were no longer copied once the synoptic Gospels began to circulate and so are lost. They are not part of the New Testament canon, the official list of Christian Scripture.

Of course, some remnants of these accounts have been incorporated into the three synoptic Gospels. This is a major reason why they are so similar. The complex problem of the literary re-

7

lationship between Matthew, Mark, and Luke is known technically as "the synoptic problem." The many facets of the problem alert us to the intense impact of Christ's coming. The Gospels do not allow us to know everything about Jesus. But they do enable us to do something more important—to know Jesus.

EVANGELIST AND GOSPEL

The term *evangelist* is related to the Greek word meaning "good news." It is found in the New Testament only three times, and always refers to preachers. Later, the term was applied to the writers of the four literary works that open the New Testament. None of the four authors refers to himself as an evangelist. In fact, none even mentions his own name as author.

How did the evangelists look upon their role in the early Christian Church?

We must answer that question in terms of the role of religious writers in the Jewish community. Authors were voices of tradition. They spoke anew the values of the received faith and invited members to celebrate revealed truth once more. A biblical writer was always a prophet, God's spokesman.

Evangelists were not merely chroniclers of past events. Their mission was to make universally available the ongoing, transforming revelation of Jesus. They created a new literary form to accomplish their task. Just as there are various literary forms such as history, fiction and the like, so the Gospels are a particular literary form or "genre" as the Scripture scholars call it. We shall discuss the genre "Gospel" in the next chapter.

For the present it is sufficient to note that the evangelists neither coined the term Gospel nor used it to describe their writings. In the New Testament the term appears most frequently in the letters of Paul to describe his teaching.

Luke does not use the word Gospel at all. Only Mark employs it as a technical term for the mission of Jesus and his Church (see

8

Mk 1.14; 14.9; 16.15). The remainder of this book will deal with basic features of the three synoptic Gospels.

Each evangelist sets the tone for his Gospel in the opening passages. As a means of orienting readers, we shall first consider the opening sections of Mark, Matthew, and Luke.

MARK'S APOCALYPTIC INTRODUCTION

Please read: Mark 1.1-13

Mark traces the "beginning of the Gospel of Jesus Christ, Son of God" to the preaching of the suffering Servant of the Lord in the book of Isaiah the prophet. Mark pictures Jesus as bringing to reality the kingdom of God long awaited by Israel. John the Baptizer in prophetic fashion invites the Jews to accept this moment of decision.

Jesus appears on the scene as God's anointed representative. He identifies with the human condition by accepting baptism. But he is more than human. As Jesus comes up out of the Jordan River, he sees the heavens split and the Holy Spirit descending as a dove upon him. A heavenly voice greets Jesus with the words, "You are my beloved Son; on you my favor rests" (1.11).

Like so much in Mark's Gospel this scene is open to many possible interpretations. Did Jesus alone see the cosmic phenomenon and hear the voice? Was it an external event or a purely inner experience?

Mark seems to describe the event in an ambiguous manner to stress that he is dealing with an apocalyptic scene, that with Jesus God's end-time is somehow already breaking into human history. Immediately after hearing this voice Jesus is "sent" by the Spirit into the desert.

In this apocalyptic no-man's-land Jesus is tempted by the Adversary, Satan (1.12-13). Mark does not go into the details of the various temptations. He wants this encounter to be seen as an end-time battle. The imagery is that of Jewish prophetic descriptions of God's kingdom. Jesus makes visible the final age of the world.

Mark's Gospel reminds readers that they will have to side either with Jesus or with the Adversary. Those who are faithful like Jesus will also experience the presence of angels and will be supported until they reach eternal life.

In Chapter III, I shall give a more detailed guide for the study of Mark's Gospel.

MATTHEW'S CONCERN FOR THE CHURCH

Please read: Matthew 1.1—4.16

Matthew prefixes to his Gospel a story of the infancy of Jesus. It has the effect of showing that even before birth, Jesus is destined to save his people, and of giving greater emphasis to the person of Jesus as chosen Messiah.

Jesus is an illustrious descendant of the royal line of David. But he is much more! His miraculous birth by the virgin mother Mary reveals him as Son of God.

Matthew uses this infancy narrative to introduce themes he will stress later in his Gospel. Jesus brings all of Scripture to its fulfillment—the Mosaic law, the prophets, the wisdom of Israel. Matthew celebrates this quality of Jesus by inserting ten "fulfillment quotations" within his text. These "fulfillment quotations" are found in Mt 1.22-23; 2.15, 17-18, 23; 4.14-16; 8.17; 12.17-21; 13.35; 21.4-5; 27.9-10.

These quotations are not spoken by Jesus. They are in the nature of editorial comments. Four of them occur in the first two chapters. Matthew identifies scenes in the earthly life of Jesus as fulfilling specific prophecies of the Old Testament.

10

USE OF RABBINICAL TECHNIQUES

In applying these texts Matthew uses rabbinical techniques unfamiliar to modern Christian readers. For example, he cites the decision of Joseph to settle in Nazareth as fulfilling "the prophets" that Jesus would be called a "Nazorean" (2.23). Yet nowhere in the Hebrew Bible is the Messiah associated with Nazareth. In fact, the city is never mentioned. Here Matthew is using the Jewish technique of playing on words to proclaim a deeper divine truth. Jesus is the Davidic *neser* (shoot) and thus the Nazorean destined to be universal savior.

By rooting Jesus in the traditions of Israel Matthew gives a distinctly Jewish character to his Gospel. He puts stress on the activity of Jesus in choosing twelve apostles and preparing them to be the foundations of the true Israel, the Church. He presents a new and radical departure from the old law, the Sermon on the Mount.

For Matthew the past is prelude. The history of Israel leads to Jesus and finds its goal in him. He fulfills the prophecy of Isaiah that an heir of David is to be born and called "Immanuel—God with us." The concern of Matthew is not the few years that Jesus was on earth but Jesus Immanuel, founder, companion and protector of his Church until the end of the world.

Jesus' choice of Capernaum as the place to start preaching fulfills the prophecy of Isaiah (8.23—9.1). He is the light that shines on a people in darkness. His Church will be the light of divine truth that will prevail over the gates of hell.

Matthew achieves an intimate binding of the earthly Jesus with the mission of his Church. He molds the figure of Jesus and the authority of the Church into one reality. Obedience to the Church is loyalty to Jesus.

11

LUKE'S PROGRAMMATIC SCENE AT NAZARETH

Please read: Luke 4.14-30

No doubt Luke was composing his Gospel about the same time as Matthew. But he wrote for a different type of people living throughout the Roman Empire. He wrote for gentile converts from paganism. They knew little about Jewish traditions and could not follow Matthew's approach.

Luke also added an infancy narrative to exalt the dignity of Jesus. He pictures Mary as the real Mount Zion receiving Jesus her Lord with joy. In his infancy narrative he never quotes Scriptur explicitly, but constantly alludes to it.

Readers of these opening chapters should use an annotated New Testament which gives the references to the Old Testament text upon which Luke builds, and then read them. This is especially true for the three great hymns of Mary, Zechariah and Simeon. They are filled with biblical imagery.

In Luke's Gospel Jesus is pictured as a hero proclaiming the king dom of God to all classes of people. Absolute loyalty to his mis sion brings Jesus into conflict with Jewish leaders and finally to his death. Luke dramatizes this rejection in the opening scene of the public life.

After his baptism Jesus returns to Nazareth. On the Sabbath th synagogue leader invites him to address the congregation. This scene operates much like a chorus in a Greek play. It gives the outline of the plot.

Jesus unfolds the biblical scroll and reads a text from Isaiah about the year of redemption. It is a time of healing and restora tion. Jesus tells the congregation that this prophecy is being fulfilled before their eyes.

His charming words enthrall the audience and they marvel at the heavenly revelation. But quickly the mood changes to one of

12

questioning. His message is too much to accept. How dare a
poor boy from their own village make such arrogant claims?
Jesus senses their doubt and counters with the proverb that a
prophet is never accepted in his home town.

The people become enraged when Jesus hints that just as they
reject him, so God may reject them. They rise up in anger and
seek to seize Jesus to kill him. Jesus walks out unharmed. Luke
uses this composite scene to foreshadow the final rejection of
Jesus on the hill of Calvary. Then he will voluntarily offer himself for the redemption of the human race.

With these introductory comments in mind readers are now ready
to analyze the nature of Gospel as a literary genre.

SUGGESTIONS FOR REFLECTION

1. At times Christians have tended to think of the Gospels basically as historical "records of the life of Jesus." What new light
is thrown on this when we alter the emphasis and refer to them
rather as "revelations of the reality of Jesus"?

2. Sometimes it is difficult for us to see a person fully when we
are close to him or her because we are so busy in day-to-day af-
fairs and caught in the emotion of the moment. Recall a person
in your life whose words or actions you only understood in retro-
spect. How might this have been the experience of the early
Christians with Jesus?

3. "Only those who have suffered for Jesus know him and the
power of his resurrection." In what way was this true of the
early assembly of believers? How did this become true for Paul?
Is it true of you in your growing relationship with Jesus?

4. Many times Paul's task of forming local churches was left in-
completed because he had to flee for his life. In our lives, too,
there are jobs, duties, responsibilities, dreams, that were inter-
rupted by unexpected events such as sickness, death, and trans-

fer. Paul's inconvenience then was a blessing for future generations because instead of speaking directly he had to write letters to continue his mission. Have your life "detours" proven a blessing for yourself and/or others?

5. Describe and define the following technical words as they relate to the Gospels: synoptic, proclaim, preach, evangelist.

6. "The Gospels do not give us complete knowledge about Jesus. But they do enable us . . . to know Jesus." What is the difference? How does this relate to the difference between "God-ward language," and "language about God"?

7. Distinguish between the three types of criticism—form criticism, tradition criticism and redaction criticism. What type of criticism does a passage like Luke 1.1-4 illustrate?

8. Recall and explain the meaning of the New Testament canon. How did this canon come to be?

9. In your letter writing what factors make the difference in the ways you correspond? The three synoptic Gospels were meant for different audiences, so the style of writing for each was different. For whom was Matthew writing? For what audience did Luke write? Why was one standard style inadequate for all? Using the introductory chapters and verses, identify some features that distinguish the writings of each: Mark, Matthew and Luke.

CHAPTER II

THE SHAPING PRINCIPLE
OF GOSPEL

We are now conscious that Christian communities existed for a whole generation before the synoptic Gospels were written. How could the Church get along without them? How necessary are they to the Christian life?

These questions force us to ask what is the identity principle of the Church. On the deepest level it is, of course, the Holy Spirit, living gift of the risen Jesus to his followers. His acting within believers guides them to comprehend, continue and celebrate the mission of their risen Lord.

BASIC ELEMENTS OF THE CHURCH

On a visible level three elements characterize the Church:
1. the special love that Christians nourish in response to Jesus' new commandment that they love one another as he did. The Holy Spirit pours that love into the hearts of believers. So this love is not of human origin, but God's personal infusion of his own life. It sustains the Church as Christ's pilgrim body in its journey to eternal union with his Father.

2. the sacramental celebrations left to the community by Jesus—especially the eucharist. That ritual meal enables believers to remember the saving death of Jesus until he comes again. The continuing representation of the last meal shared by Jesus and his disciples, and his final sacrifice on the cross, provides the means

of keeping the Church faithful to the mind and mission of the Lord.

3. the unique authority that Jesus enjoyed as God's beloved So He communicated this to his apostles so that they could speak f him and act in his name. The Gospels arose out of this gift.

The first two elements are not limited in time or place. But the authority of the apostles was bound up with their temporary ex istence on earth. As they grew older they sensed the need to hand on to the community an authoritative account of the reve tion of Jesus. In a very real sense the canonical Gospels replace the apostolic presence within the Church.

Each generation of believers must turn to the Gospels to be instructed as to who Jesus is. The Church never celebrates the eu charistic meal without reading from a Gospel. This brings an ap ostolic presence to every liturgy. Christians affirm confidently in the creed their belief in "one, holy, catholic and apostolic Church."

GOSPELS ARE CULT PROCLAMATIONS

Individual Christians often read and reflect on Gospel scenes in private meditation. Yet their primary role in the Church is to deepen its common faith and sacramental life. Gospels reveal what we celebrate in sacrament and prepare believers to interior ize the mystery of Jesus.

The Gospels have power to do this because they preserve an inspired account of God's self-revelation in the earthly life of Jesus. They express the early Church's understanding that God makes himself available in Jesus in a new way.

To appreciate this function of the Gospels, recall the appearanc of God in the Old Testament to persons like Abraham and Mos Those favored by such a vision would commemorate the occasic by erecting some kind of memorial shrine. Pilgrims would com

16

there to celebrate the theophany or divine appearance, and thus it became a special place of cult, that is, of worship.

On anniversaries of the appearance, a group of worshipers would assemble to celebrate. The leader of the cult, usually a priest, recited what God had done for his people at this sanctuary. This was the "sacred word" or cult proclamation. Such ceremonies renewed fervor in the hearts of Israel, and made real and present the past event now being celebrated.

In Jesus God appeared in a new kind of theophany—not in momentary vision but as incarnate Savior. His whole life was a visible revelation of God's saving love. Jesus made available to believers the power to draw divine life into their existence; to be transformed into children of God.

This is why I stress that a Gospel is a special kind of literature, a divine revelation rather than human teaching. By their very nature, the Gospels are short because they center in on the words and deeds that communicate God's saving love through Jesus and are not concerned with details irrelevant to their message. It follows that the Gospels could originate only within a believing community. They remain a question mark to outsiders. They constantly challenge believers who hear them to pursue the values Jesus celebrated.

Before studying an individual Gospel believers need to have an overview of its individual unity. The rest of this chapter deals with the big picture. It seeks to broaden the horizons of readers so they can grasp each Gospel as a unified whole. These pages will prepare for reading the individual Gospels of Matthew, Mark and Luke.

OVERVIEW OF A GOSPEL

The first feature to grasp about a Gospel is its overarching unity. Each Gospel is meant to be read as a literary unit. All elements within the whole are Gospel. They take on characteristics of the author's theological point of view.

The literary genre of Gospel possesses great simplicity. A prayerful reader is quickly able to grasp the interconnection of its various parts. All its elements have as their focal point the mission of Jesus. His mission, in turn, is the climax of a long series of divine revelations in the world.

Jesus did not appear out of nowhere. He was son of Abraham, son of David. What is more, he was son of the God of Abraham. Long ago the God of the Heavenly Hosts called Abraham to be father of a great nation. The fate of that nation appears in the sacred writings of the Jews.

As a Jew, Jesus studied these writings, prayed over them, loved them. They helped shape his human consciousness and religious experience. He proclaimed his loyalty to the law of Moses. But Jesus felt free to adapt that law, even to reinterpret it. As a result even his followers found it difficult to understand his divine mission.

When God did not rescue Jesus and he died for his mission, his followers were at a loss. Even after his resurrection they were not clear as to what they should do.

The apostles turned to the Old Testament for guidance. And they began to see Jesus everywhere. They found terms and images capable of serving as vehicles for communicating their faith. They celebrated God's work in Jesus first by their preaching and eventually in written form in Gospels.

Efforts to proclaim Jesus relied heavily upon Greek translations of the Hebrew Bible then in use among Hellenistic Jews. These were Jews living among pagans. They adopted the Greek language and a modified Greek culture. But they also developed a vocabulary of special terms or gave new meanings to existing words to express their faith.

18

Even this vocabulary was not capable of expressing fully the mystery of Jesus. Under the guidance of the Holy Spirit the early Church saw that Jesus was a man "who fits no formula." He reconciled on a deeper level apparent contradictions found among the oracles of the prophets and the demands of the law. He surpassed all previous personages and development of events of salvation history.

JESUS AS UNIQUE SON

Among the many Gospel narratives that convey the truth of the unique mission of Jesus, we may select the parable of the wicked vineyardists (Mk 12.1-8). The chosen people killed the servants, the prophets, who came from God. Now they have killed even the son of the owner of the vineyard, Jesus.

Obviously, it took the followers of Jesus many years and a wide variety of experiences to work out a comprehensive portrait of Jesus as the only-begotten Son of God. Thanks to the guiding presence of the Holy Spirit they came to a deep appreciation of the saving plan of God. It comes to fulfillment not only in the earthly Jesus but also in the community he prepared by his life.

Only out of long years of preaching, setting up local communities and overcoming opposition did the shaping principle of the literary genre Gospel come into being.

The uniqueness of this new literary creation springs less from its contents than from the flow and interaction of its elements. I will present these elements now. Knowledge of them will enable readers to enter more actively into dialogue with the heart of the New Testament.

THE SHAPING PRINCIPLE OF GOSPEL

We can safely say that the Gospel of Mark represents the most primitive expression of Gospel form. It lacks the more developed features of both Matthew and Luke, such as infancy narrative and extended sermon material. But Mark does contain all the elements necessary to be a true Gospel.

Most modern New Testament commentators attribute to Mark the creation of this truly new literary genre. A new literary mode of expression was necessary to express the radically new work of Jesus. Mark's work was new but it would have been impossible without a great number of previous steps.

We saw that it took the believing Christian community a whole generation to grasp adequately the dignity and the mission of Jesus. Only then was it possible to make a transition of his revelation into a literary genre. What Mark had to do was to filter out of a vast amount of material the key moments in the mission of Jesus.

The organization of these key elements forms the shaping principle of Gospel genre. These are five, namely:

(1) God's calling of Jesus to be Messiah. This is portrayed through events surrounding his baptism. Through a voice from heaven the Father reveals to Jesus that he has been anointed for his role as proclaimer of the kingdom of God. Jesus is filled with the Holy Spirit to announce the good news.

(2) the testing of God's Son. Jesus must pass through a test before he can assume his mission of introducing the kingdom. Unlike Adam, the first-born of creation, Jesus proves loyal and rebuffs Satan. He begins to initiate the new creation.

(3) the revelation of the kingdom of God in word and deed. The major part of the Gospels portrays how Jesus bore witness to the saving power of God working within him. He manifested the kingdom by both his words of wisdom and his mighty deeds that reinforced each other. I shall discuss his principal forms of revelation, parables and miracles, in Chapters VI and VII.

(4) the rejection of Jesus by his own people. Jesus shattered the preconceived notions of contemporary Jewish leaders by the way he manifested the will of God. His consciousness of being God's Son shocked them. He claimed an authority beyond the law of Moses and the temple of Jerusalem. When his claims were resisted, Jesus did not alter his approach. On the contrary, he insisted that God was purifying the spirit of his people. His loyalty to his vision culminated in the passion and death, which the Gospels treat at length. I shall discuss them in Chapter VIII.

(5) the resurrection of Jesus. His enemies did not have the last word. They crucified Jesus but the Father raised him to life. Gospel genre ends in the area of new life and hope. Chapter IX will treat this important element that helped shape the principle of Gospel.

EXAMPLE OF MARK'S APPROACH

Please read: Mark 6.6—8.30

A great variety of materials celebrating the words and deeds of Jesus circulated in early Christian communities. But the spark of Mark's genius was needed to capture the uniqueness of the mission of Jesus in unified literary form. His creation of the Gospel genre still touches every believer. Thanks to him it is impossible to imagine Jesus in any other way than as the Messiah who freely chose the cross in obedience to his Father's plan of salvation.

Mark created this literary unity out of existing oral and written traditions he received from earlier stages of the apostolic preaching. Thus his Gospel manifests tension between community tradition and personal insight. His method is to bring together past events and the ongoing response of faith.

This demand for faith involves Mark's readers in the universal saving work of Jesus through the Church. An essential dimension of Gospel genre is to bring readers to decision with respect to the Christ event.

21

Mark's technique to gain reader involvement is his use of cyclic patterns. The first half of his Gospel is arranged in three cycles. It indicates that Jesus called to conversion not once but many times. Each cycle begins with a scene involving the disciples (Mk 1.16; 3.13; 6.7). All three end on a note of misunderstanding—a hint at the final rejection of Jesus by those to whom he preached.

The last of these cycles is especially interesting to show how Mark used tradition. The events narrated appear in pairs. Jesus multiplies loaves twice. He crosses the lake twice. He engages in controversy twice and works a miracle twice.

MARK'S USE OF TRADITION

This repetition of the same pattern of events points to Mark's method of working with oral tradition. Most probably both cycles come from oral tradition—one from the Jewish Christian part of the Church, the other from converts from paganism. The events go back to scenes from the earthly life of Jesus that were meaningful to both groups of believers.

In the course of oral evangelization details of the multiplication of the loaves were modified. Preachers adapted them to customs within local communities. At the time of writing Mark chooses to incorporate both the Jewish Christian and the converted pagan cycles into his Gospel. His interest extends beyond the past deed of Jesus to its present teaching value. This miracle helps believers relate better to the powerful presence of Jesus in the eucharist.

Into this last cycle Mark inserts the story of a blind man whose cure by Jesus was gradual. Only Mark preserves this unusual scene (8.22-26). It is no doubt symbolic of the slow and almost painful growth in faith by Peter and the other disciples.

This gradual cure anticipates the lack of understanding of Peter in his "confession" that follows immediately (8.27-30). Mark paints it as a misunderstanding of Jesus. Peter would have turned Jesus into a political Messiah.

Jesus rejects this approach and rebukes Peter as Satan. But he does not reject Peter. In fact, Mark will picture Jesus spending the rest of his ministry preparing his disciples to accept God's saving plan on a spiritual level.

THE RESURRECTION NARRATIVE

As I explained earlier, interest in events of the earthly life of Jesus developed relatively late in the Christian community. Among all New Testament writings these events are narrated only in the Gospels. Even here only a relatively small amount of material has survived.

The evangelists retain only enough of the earthly words and deeds of Jesus to portray God revealing himself through him. Their emphasis is upon Jesus' suffering and rejection at the hands of those who refused to receive him as Messiah.

All Gospels contrast divine approval and human rejection at work in the life of Jesus. By human standards his life ends in failure to convince his people about his mission. If Jesus had to be measured by what happened before his death he would simply be remembered as a tragic figure.

The heart of the Gospels is to proclaim that Jesus cannot be boxed in or evaluated by human standards. Without his resurrection no Gospel could exist.

The reality of Jesus extends beyond the life he gave for others. Jesus is the risen one who goes before the believing Church as its living Lord. Believers live in the tension between his unselfish death and his future coming in glory.

The earliest and best manuscripts of Mark's Gospel end with the abrupt sentence about the women who found that Jesus' body was not in the tomb. They saw only a young man sitting inside. He told them to tell the disciples and especially Peter that Jesus had gone to Galilee. They would meet him there. But the women were overcome with religious ecstasy and fled in silence. They told no one, "For they were afraid" (Mk 16.8).

Such an abrupt ending naturally invited copyists to add a more rounded out conclusion. Three of these are well known, but they are obviously later summaries. (See the *New American Bible,* Mk 16.9-20, and the conclusions called "The Shorter Ending" and "The Freer Logion.")

Mark wants his readers to recognize that the resurrection of Jesus is not over. It is an ongoing mystery constantly challenging believers to quest for their Lord. In a word, Gospel is ultimately about discipleship.

DISCIPLESHIP–THE GOSPEL CALL

Please read: Luke 22.24-38

The Gospels are not simply about the mission of Jesus in the past. They affirm that his existence shapes the life of every believer. Jesus is the only person who entered the world voluntarily. He came to relate to others and to achieve a new relation between all humanity and his Father.

The Gospels were written long after Jesus died. But his work on earth is responsible for their existence. Jesus chose special companions to associate with him. He communicated his unique sense of mission to them. They never really understood him and one eventually betrayed him. Even their chosen leader denied Jesus during his trial.

Just before the tragic end Luke inserts into the Last Supper narrative an instructive exchange between Jesus and his twelve chosen disciples. It is his final word about leadership in the community of believers. To create the scene Luke refers to a dispute that has taken place on the road to Jerusalem after James and John requested the best posts in his kingdom (Mk 10.41-45).

Luke has the quarrel flare up within the Last Supper. Jesus reacts by telling them about how much more mature contemporary pagan leaders were. They went to the ethical philosophers to learn. They were told they must be benefactors of their subjects and patronize them. Surely a logical approach.

Jesus then takes a surprising turn. This was not the kind of leadership he wanted among his followers. Those aspiring to be leaders must become servants of all. Their model is the great act of Jesus in humbling himself and becoming obedient to the cross.

Such a demand is terrifying. Jesus knows that. So he turns to Peter, the leader of the apostles, and assures him that he prays for him and will not abandon him.

Then Jesus addresses all the apostles. He reminds them of his past support. They lacked nothing when he sent them out to preach. Now they must prepare themselves for even greater opposition and for a more arduous mission.

With these general features of Gospel in mind, we can turn to the writings of the individual evangelists. Each one developed the Gospel genre to meet the needs of the growing Church.

SUGGESTIONS FOR REFLECTION

1. In what ways might you identify a believing and practicing Catholic to a nonbeliever? How do the Gospels relate to these beliefs and practices? How does your list compare with the three ways the Church is characterized in this chapter?

2. What is "cult proclamation"? Why are the Gospels called "cult proclamations"? Why are Gospel episodes usually short?

Compared to unbelievers, why are believers better able to understand and accept the Gospels?

3. How did the "roots" of Jesus shape his human consciousness and religious experience? In what ways did he depart from his roots? How did the Scriptures of the Old Testament help the apostles understand more fully who Jesus was and what his mission was? Why is the same thing true for us today?

4. What is a "literary genre"? How and when did the literary genre "Gospel" come to be? In what ways is this genre unique?

5. If you had to summarize the key moments or elements in the mission of Jesus, with which ones would you identify? What were the key moments that Mark highlighted when he wrote his Gospel?

6. "An essential dimension of Gospel genre is to bring readers to decision with respect to the Christ event." Having read Mark 1.16, Mark 3.13, and Mark 6.6-8, what decisions do you see that the apostles had to make in these episodes? With what decisions are you, the reader, faced in the same passages? Is it your usual practice to consider a decision after reading a passage of Scripture?

7. Point to specific occasions in Mark's Gospel which reflect: 1) the oral traditions of his times, 2) application to the present of a teaching value in the past deeds of Jesus, 3) symbolic actions and words (i.e., deeper or hidden meanings represented by obvious deeds and words).

8. Throughout history Christians have emphasized different aspects of the life of Jesus at different periods. What aspects of the life of Jesus do you tend to favor? Since the overall emphasis in each Gospel is on "the divine approval and human rejection at work in the life of Jesus," how do the events selected by you reflect this emphasis?

9. Having read Luke 22.24-38 and Mark 10.41-45, what discoveries have you made about the life of discipleship? In reflection on your own life as a disciple, which of these have you personally experienced?

10. "Leaders must become servants of all." How have you found this to be generally true in your dealings with leaders in families, business, education, government, the Church?

CHAPTER III

MARK'S PORTRAIT OF
THE MESSIAH

The infant Christian Church faced one of its most serious crises about one generation after the death of Jesus. The original eye witnesses to his earthly life were now old. They could no longe preach and teach. Who was to guide the destiny of this religiou movement?

True, the Holy Spirit remains its transcendent guide. But earthi authority is needed as a sign to unify, stabilize and provide lead ership. As we saw in Chapter II, the Church had three gifts fror Jesus to maintain its vigor. These are: his command to love on another as he loved, the sacrament of the eucharist, and apostol ic authority.

GOSPELS PROLONG APOSTOLIC AUTHORITY

In one sense an apostle's authority could not be transmitted. It was linked to a personal choice by Jesus and actual contact with him during his ministry (see Acts 1.21-22). Yet, the use of a written narrative provided a means to transmit the apostolic understanding of the person and mission of Jesus to future gen- erations in a stable and authoritative form.

To Peter's disciple, Mark, was given the inspiration to produce a carefully constructed written narrative embodying the heart of

Jesus' revelation. Mark was the first person in the Church to create a Gospel. He fashioned an account of the words and deeds of Jesus extending from his baptism by John to his resurrection.

This Gospel is a marvelous blend of traditional materials taught by the apostles and an organizing form developed by Mark. The enduring significance for believers of every age flows from Mark's theological insight.

Jesus emerges from the Gospel not as another religious hero of a past age. He shines forth as living Lord and Messiah. Through his obedience to the Father's will on the cross Jesus entered into heavenly glory and is still with us.

SEEING MARK'S GOSPEL AS A WHOLE

Most Catholics come into contact with the Gospels at their liturgical celebrations. These are the public worship of the Church. The presiding priest reads the small section ordered by the Church for each particular day. He then preaches a homily related in some way to the text.

The end result is that many believers have a passing acquaintance with the Gospels but not a living knowledge of them. They can recall scenes and striking phrases. But they cannot see the overall movement of the drama or how each individual scene is somehow good news of salvation for them.

Mark has carefully organized apostolic traditions available to him to proclaim an important truth. We cannot accept Jesus as Savior except in terms of God's plan.

Mark goes even further. His insight is to proclaim that the hearing of the good news is possible only in an attitude of discipleship. Jesus came not to be served but to serve and to offer his life as "ransom" for the many (Mk 10.45).

PARADOXICAL SECRET IN MARK

Please read: Mark 3.7-12

The reader soon runs into an apparent contradiction. Mark presents Jesus as working wonders. But then he commands persons he helps not to tell anyone. This paradox constitutes the so-called "messianic secret" of Mark's Gospel. Where does it come from? What is the reason for it?

Once we accept Mark as a true author, we recognize that obviously he was writing for believers living at least a generation after the death of Jesus. This messianic secret was part of Mark's theology. It was his way of warning believers against relating to Jesus primarily as a wonder worker.

To see Jesus primarily in terms of working miracles is to misunderstand his mission. It destroys the real nature of discipleship. It would turn the Church into an elitist group. Only those possessing extraordinary charism could claim to be authentic Christians.

Without his revelation of God's saving love through cross redemption Jesus is not the good news of salvation to all.

IDENTIFYING WITH THE APOSTLES

Please read: Mark 1.14—3.12

The role played by the disciples of Jesus is an essential part of Mark's literary and theological presentation. He carefully arranged the materials he used from tradition into patterns. These patterns invite readers to enter into the condition of discipleship. Jesus calls his followers to faith and service.

Mark groups the material of the first half of his Gospel into three cycles having the same pattern. The scenes he chooses contrast Jesus' efforts to save with resistance to his gift.

Each pattern begins with a brief summary of the ministry of

Jesus. He preaches the good news of God (see Mk 1.14-15). He affirms that the reign of God for which John the Baptizer and the prophets of old had prepared the people is now at hand.

Immediately follows a scene featuring his disciples (see Mk 1. 16-20). Jesus calls his first disciples along the shore of the Lake of Galilee. There are two sets of brothers—Simon and Andrew, James and John.

By the time of the second summary Mark pictures Jesus as surrounded by people from all parts of the Holy Land. Even pagans from Tyre and Sidon are coming to him because of his miraculous healing power (see Mk 3.7-12).

In this setting Jesus appoints twelve apostles to be special companions in his ministry. They share his mission of proclaiming the kingdom of God by driving out demons and by other mighty deeds (see Mk 3.13-19).

The third summary in Mark 6.6 is quite brief. It simply pictures Jesus as going around preaching in villages. Another scene with disciples follows. Jesus sends his twelve special followers forth to evangelize. He demands a spirit of detachment from material things. Their trust is to be in God alone. Their mission is to call to repentance, to heal and to drive out demons.

At this point Mark creates a sense of lapsed time by inserting the story of how John the Baptizer was murdered (6.14-29). Then he pictures the Twelve returning to report on their mission to Jesus. This is the only place they are called apostles in Mark's Gospel (6.30).

In these three cycles the scenes with disciples are followed by narratives about Jesus. He is occupied with his mission of revealing the reign of God by miraculous deeds and by his teaching. In all three cases the result is resistance and rejection by his own people.

Mark's care in arranging his material becomes evident to the reader. He contrasts the fidelity of Jesus to reveal the reign of God and the poor response to his message. Thus Mark already intimates the final rejection of Jesus.

CONTROVERSY IN MARK

Even the chosen disciples of Jesus fail to understand. But they are willing to learn. For all their weakness they stand in opposition to the organized religious authority that is continually stirring up controversy with Jesus.

The opposition accuses Jesus of being in league with devils and of possessing an unclean spirit (Mk 3.22, 30). Jesus in turn warn his disciples against the "leaven of the Pharisees," the hypocrisy that blinds them. They refuse the saving power of God working in and through Jesus.

The rejection of the earthly Jesus will also have its counterpart in the Christian community. All readers need to heed the advice that Jesus gave to disciples who wanted signs about the future, "Watch out for yourselves" (Mk 13.9).

PETER'S CONFESSION AND THE CROSS

Please read: Mark 8.27-33

Mark deliberately creates suspense. Jesus constantly reveals the reign of God but his hearers invariably misunderstand. This suspense reaches a climax in the response of Peter and the other disciples to the question of Jesus' identity.

Jesus takes them into the territory of Caesarea Philippi, a pagan area north of Galilee. The purpose of this departure from the strictly Jewish territory becomes clear from Jesus' questions. What are people saying about him? All answers show radical misunderstanding. Jesus is identified as a figure from the past— John the Baptizer or some prophet.

What about the disciples? Who is Jesus for them?

As spokesman Peter affirms the belief of all. Jesus is the Christ, the Messiah, Israel's anointed king! It looks like the suspense is over. Jesus has finally met true faith.

But no! Jesus responds in an unusual way. First of all, they are to tell no one. If Jesus had stopped there, we might say he was confirming Peter's answer. He simply wanted them to keep this a secret until he was ready for a public display. Then they could share their faith with others.

But Jesus adds a second part to his answer. He starts to unfold the future. The remainder of his life will be marked by greater opposition, by rejection by his own people, even by a cruel death. But God will not abandon him.

At this point Peter betrays his lack of real faith. He takes Jesus aside and warns him about speaking that way. He will destroy his chances of winning acceptance as messianic king in Jerusalem. In other words, Peter had projected his own image of the Messiah as a military ruler upon Jesus. He expected Jesus to drive the Romans out by force.

Jesus' angry reply unmasks Peter as "satan." Rather than a disciple he is a tempter seeking to draw Jesus from obedience to the Father.

Mark's graphic portrayal of this confrontation dramatizes the central message of the Gospel. Salvation comes only as a divine gift and only through cross redemption. This scene is the turning point in Mark's Gospel.

From then on Jesus concentrates on teaching his disciples. He shows them the role of the cross in their salvation. Not only must Jesus accept the cross but every disciple must embrace it also. This scene becomes an encouragement to every believer who reads Mark. Faith is always a struggle, but Jesus is at hand to provide the strength needed for victory.

THE PASSION PREDICTIONS

Please read: Mark 8.31–9.1; 9.33-37; 10.35-45

A new pattern begins with Jesus' first prediction of his passion. Not once, but three times Jesus predicts that he will suffer rejection by his own people. He will be betrayed by them to pagan authorities. But God will show approval of his mission by raising him up to glory.

The repetition of these predictions serves a double purpose. It points out that the early Church struggled to come to terms with the scandal of the cross. It keeps reminding believers they have to constantly wrestle with this truth.

What Mark insists upon in narrating these predictions is their link to discipleship. The cross serves to identify not only Jesus but his followers. The apostles resisted this mark of identity. But Jesus responds after each prophecy with a short discourse on discipleship in terms of dying to self.

The first of these discourses consists of only six sentences. But they are arranged in a concentric pattern: ABCC'B'A' (Mk 8. 34–9.1). This arrangement unifies all these statements into a forceful proclamation of the centrality of the cross.

The condition of being a disciple of Jesus is to accept the pattern of the cross as a lifestyle. The cross broadens the horizons of believers into those of Jesus. They make their decisions according to God's will rather than this world's values. Just as Jesus was willing to lay down his life for others so must those who wish to share his glory prefer Gospel values to their own lives.

THE SON OF MAN

A phrase found frequently in connection with the passion is "Son of Man." Up to this point it occurred only twice in Mark (2.10, 28). It is an Old Testament phrase used often by the prophet Ezekiel. This Hebrew phrase had no real meaning in Greek, just as it has no meaning in English.

Some translations render it as "human being." The difficulty with that choice is to make modern readers miss all the biblical allusions built into the title.

The term Son of Man seems to have grown out of historical situations. As the Israelites came into greater contact with pagan nations, they reflected more on their special role in world history. How did they fit into God's plan? On the historical level they were oppressed and exiled. They started to dream of a better future. God would intervene dramatically and make them rulers over the pagans.

AN APOCALYPTIC TITLE

The title Son of Man is prominent in a Jewish book from the second century before Christ, the Book of Daniel. It paints a heavenly Son of Man coming on clouds and receiving from God authority and glory and universal royal power (Dan 7.13-14). It belongs to a class of literature called apocalyptic, that is, writing that reveals future ages.

Mark characterizes Jesus as an apocalyptic figure. He came to introduce the new age of God's reign. By calling Jesus the Son of Man, Mark proclaims that the sufferings of Jesus are not failure but the pangs of a new age. Jesus will return on clouds of glory.

LINK BETWEEN SUFFERINGS AND GLORY

It is time to speak of the other two predictions of the passion. Jesus shows his disciples that his glory can never be separated from his sufferings. The second prediction is made as if the betrayal has already taken place (Mk 9.31). Jesus knew of his rejection. Yet his disciples did not "know" what he was saying.

Mark paints them as selfish. They vie with one another for the best positions. So Jesus gives them another short talk on discipleship. It means becoming servant of all. In serving even the little child they are serving him (9.37).

The third prediction of the passion comes after Peter boasts they have left everything to follow Jesus (10.28). The reply of Jesus has a touch of irony. Those who have left what is dearest to them on a human level—family and possessions—for Jesus and the Gospel will be rewarded a hundredfold even in this life. Then he adds, "and persecutions besides." Eternal life will follow in due time.

To endure persecution is one dimension of the cross of being a disciple. Jesus lists it among the good gifts. Then he reinforces his message by starting to head for Jerusalem. He is willing to undergo the cross that awaits him.

In this tense setting Jesus gives a detailed description of the sufferings awaiting him. The response of two close disciples is astonishing. James and John approach Jesus with a special request. Let them have the first places in his kingdom!

All Jesus can promise them and every disciple is a share in his suffering. For the Son of Man came not to receive service but to lay down his life as a "ransom" in place of many (10.45). To accept this role is the condition for being exalted by the Father when Jesus returns in glory.

TENSIONS BETWEEN CHRIST'S GOING AND RETURN

Please read: Mark 11.1—13.37

Another way Mark reveals the centrality of the cross is to devote about a third of his Gospel to the final week of the life of Jesus. His three passion predictions have prepared readers for the unfolding of these tragic events.

Even in the midst of plots against his life Jesus does not lose his sense of mission. He remains confident that God's power will bring the kingdom to fulfillment. He warns his disciples against losing confidence and courage by cursing the fig tree that had leaves but no fruit—a symbol of Israel (11.12-20).

When his opponents try to trap him Jesus counters with his own challenge: How can the Messiah be both David's son and David's Lord (12.35-37)?

Before allowing himself to be taken Jesus delivers a farewell sermon to his disciples. It takes the form of a revelation about the final days of this age. That is the so-called apocalyptic discourse (13.5-37). The term itself means "revelation." Implied is that this type of literature centers on the intervention of God to judge his creation and bring it to its completion.

For modern Americans this sermon is difficult to follow. The apocalyptic style is foreign to our modern scientific and historically conditioned minds. It cannot be forced into our thought categories. It is a rejection of all forms of worldly wisdom that seek to control human destiny.

THE REVELATION OF THE END

The occasion for this sermon is the disciples' amazement at the magnificence of the temple of Jerusalem. Jesus replies that the whole thing will be destroyed completely.

The three leading disciples, Peter, James and John, approach Jesus privately for more information about this. Mark shows Jesus leading them over to the Mount of Olives across the valley from the city. He sits and delivers this difficult and highly symbolic account of the last days.

On the one hand, the end seems to be very close—so be on your guard against deception (13.5). Yet the end must be far into the future. Before it comes the Gospel must be preached to the world (13.10).

The discourse continues along this paradoxical vein. It is an image of the future facing the Church. On the one hand, God is always near and worthy of absolute trust. Yet God is always beyond our reach and never subject to our control. The Church must live in vivid expectancy of God's transforming coming. Their hope is on the watch. Their faith prevents them from compromising with the world.

By inserting this apocalyptic discourse right before the story of the passion of Jesus, Mark puts the death of Jesus and his return in glory on the same level. The Church derives life from both the death of Jesus and his parousia, that is, his return in glory.

Believers must be prepared for persecution, suffering, even cosmic upheavals. Only after that will the Son of Man return in glory with angels as ministers.

By putting these predictions in this mysterious, symbolic form, Jesus warns his followers against trying to figure out and control these events. God alone knows the time. The believer's task is to be awake, to watch in faith.

THE CHURCH NEEDS THE GOSPELS

In one sense this great apocalyptic discourse of the Gospel of Mark helps us understand why Gospels were composed. The

Church always needs guidance from the apostles' wisdom to nourish its gift of faith, its mutual love and its hope to share in victory of its Lord. No matter how long this period of waiting lasts, it is still the final age of God's saving plan.

The revelation of Jesus—his teaching and his example—will always remain the guide and norm for the Church's life.

The Gospel of Mark invites the Christian community in this world to face up to its responsibility with the same loyalty as Jesus accepted his mission. Believers bear the cross with confidence and childlike simplicity. Every believer must walk the path of Christ's passion. It is not a blind alley but the gateway to freedom and eternal life.

SUGGESTIONS FOR REFLECTION

1. What is the "messianic secret" in Mark's Gospel? What is its meaning for us today? Do you think it is necessary for our times?

2. What were some of the stipulations Jesus placed on his disciples as he sent them out to evangelize? How can these have meaning for us as disciples today?

3. What was the great error that Jesus referred to as " the leaven of the Pharisees"?

4. Mark was writing for Christians of the first century. Why was the advice of Jesus to his disciples in Mark 13.9 important for the readers?

5. Read again Mark 8.27-30 and try to answer it for yourself, as though Jesus were asking you.

6. How does the scene in Mark 8.27-33 reflect the central message of the Gospel? Why can this be called the turning point of Mark's Gospel?

7. When Jesus speaks of the cross as the sign of a disciple, what does he mean about life? How does this compare or contrast with the meaning of cross as you were taught it?

8. Apocalyptic style is used in Mark's Gospel to teach a powerful lesson about the meaning of life. What is the lesson found in Mark 13.5-37? Should its descriptive passages be taken literally? Is the passage true? What relationship has it for us today? for your own personal life? Do you know any other examples of apocalyptic writing in literature?

CHAPTER IV

LUKE HUMANIZES THE MESSAGE

The call of St. Paul to faith was one of the turning points in the early Church's growth. By background Paul was a Pharisee. He wrote that he had been so zealous for the law of Moses that he persecuted the followers of Jesus.

His conversion brought about a crucial change in his attitude toward the law. He recognized that it could not save.

Paul spent his Christian missionary career sharing his new insight. His approach brought him into conflict not only with believing Jews but with many Christian Jews as well. They wished to maintain customs from the law. Paul vehemently opposed that approach. Christ broke down all barriers between human beings and created one new Body, the Church.

One of the followers and companions of Paul was Luke. Paul calls him a "co-worker" (Phlm 24). Second Timothy, a kind of last will and testimony of Paul, states that only Luke was with the imprisoned Paul (4.11).

WITNESS TO PAUL'S WORK

Luke himself tells us that he was not a companion of the earthly Jesus. He depends on "eyewitnesses and ministers of the word" for accuracy and on Paul for his theology (1.2). Paul has evidently died before Luke writes his Gospel because he dedicates his work to Theophilus.

41

It may seem strange that Luke should write a Gospel. He was not an apostle and probably not even a Jew. Yet he had special qualifications for assuming this role. As Paul's disciple he learned the "word of the cross" from missionary experience. He saw the saving power of the good news bring healing to converted pagans and endow them with every form of spiritual gift.

Luke watched the flexibility of the Gospel message. It brought good news to all types of people in every level of society. His background made him sensitive to the needs of converts from paganism. He knew the kind of encouragement they needed to undertake a lifestyle more demanding than the permissive moral standards of the Hellenistic world.

From his study of Greek history and literature Luke knew how pagans developed codes of personal ethics. Homer was still the textbook of young aristocrats. Society at large learned standards of conduct from the great tragedies performed at the annual festivals.

These festivals had both religious and social dimensions. The character flaws in their tragic heroes aroused an emotional purification in the spectators. In theory this katharsis led to a more noble life.

Close to the time of Jesus there also flourished "kingship tracts." These were ethical guides for members of the ruling class. They set up moral standards for personal maturity, social activity and community justice.

The audience Luke addressed needed to see Jesus as a moral hero to be respected and worshiped. Without such an example these converts from Hellenistic philosophy or popular pagan cults would find difficulty in sustaining the high ideals of their new Christian faith. Once they were convinced that Jesus was alive and present and interested in them, they would respond to the challenges he offered.

Luke did not make the mistake of equating Jesus with other popular heroes. His Gospel enters into dialogue with Greek culture and maintains a tension between revelation and reason. If he compares Jesus with Greek heroes, he also contrasts them.

Jesus is Lord in a unique, transcendent sense. He is God's Son. As a result, believers are both liberated and enslaved by him. Jesus is more powerful and more compassionate that humans can imagine. His demands are also more far reaching than any human power could impose.

LUKE MODIFIES THE GOSPEL GENRE

Please read: Luke 1.26-38

Like the other evangelists, Luke is representative of the apostolic Church. His task is not to change tradition but to adapt it to the changing needs of ever-expanding groups of Christians. His audience embraces cultured Greek-speaking members who knew no Hebrew. They had little interest in the niceties of Jewish law and social customs.

Luke accepts the overall direction Mark gave to Gospel form. His modifications are not significant enough to create a distinct form of literature. Like that of Mark, his Gospel is a revelation inviting prayerful reflection and response.

By meditating upon Luke's special themes and modifications believers come to a personal appreciation of the person and mission of Jesus. Some of the principal interests evident in Luke's Gospel are:

(1) to exalt the person of Jesus. This concern is evident in Luke's infancy narrative. Jesus appears as "great" and "Son of the Most High" and king of Israel (1.32). When his mother visits her cousin Elizabeth, she is greeted as "the mother of my Lord" (1.43).

Luke features the title Lord for Jesus. His disciples give it to
him. Luke wants his readers to understand Lord in the strongest
sense—as universal Ruler of heaven and earth. Jesus is more
than a Hellenistic benefactor.

(2) to present the Holy Spirit as guiding the earthly Jesus. Luke
uses the term Holy Spirit more frequently than the other evangelists. He comes upon Mary to effect the conception of Jesus
(1.35). The baptism of Jesus is a descent of the Holy Spirit.
Then Jesus, filled by him, is led into the desert to undergo temp-
tation (4.1). Jesus rejoices in the Holy Spirit when he sees his
disciples driving out unclean spirits (10.21).

(3) to present followers of Jesus as his slaves. When the angel
tells Mary her predestined role as mother of Jesus, she responds,
"Behold the Lord's slave girl" (1.37). In her hymn of praise she
thanks God for looking upon the lowliness of his slave girl (1.48).

Mary's response corresponds to what Luke observed in the life
of Paul. He too saw himself as slave of the Lord Jesus. When
the aged Simeon took Jesus in his arms, he recognized him as
God's gift of salvation. He too identifies himself as slave. The
word is to be understood in the religious sense found in the Old
Testament. It proclaims salvation as gift of God's compassion.

Jesus urges his followers to cultivate this attitude in the parable
of the slave returning late from working in the fields. After
working all day he still has to get his master's supper—and think
nothing of it. No human can put God under obligation. "We
are all useless slaves" (17.10).

(4) to show the saving power of faith. Luke records four occasions when Jesus says to people he cured, "Your faith has saved
you" (7.50; 8.48; 17.19; 18.42). The faith of Zacchaeus draws
Jesus into his home. Only by faith do we benefit by the coming
of the Son of Man "to seek and save what was lost" (19.10).

LUKE'S JOURNEY NARRATIVE

Please read: Luke 9.51–13.35

The most striking literary feature of Luke's Gospel is his so-called "great addition" (9.51–18.14). After the events centering around Jesus' second prediction of his passion, Luke interrupts the order of Mark's Gospel. He inserts a long series of scenes and teachings that enrich knowledge of Jesus.

From the viewpoint of sources, this section points to at least one written source besides the Markan tradition. The piece is called Q from the German word for spring or source, Quelle. Both Matthew and Luke used it but in different ways.

Following his goal of an orderly account, Luke organized his materials into artistic units, often by themes. At times the unity is purely literary. For example, the banquet setting serves to unite the stories of Chapter 14.

The theme dominating the great Lukan addition is Jesus' going up to Jerusalem. Luke's aim is not to chronicle stages of an actual historical journey. The movement is fundamentally theological (see 13.22, 33; 17.11). Jesus "sets his face to go to Jerusalem." He does this because the "days of his ascension are fulfilled" (9.51).

The mysterious opening verse of this addition calls attention to the symbolic journey Jesus is taking. It will lead not merely to the material city but to his heavenly Father.

Jesus knows what awaits him at Jerusalem. The parable of the barren fig tree bears witness to the failure of Israel to bear the fruit of faith in him (13.6-9). This parable contains the same message as the cursing of the fig tree in Mk 11.12-14.

In this section Luke includes the warning a group of Pharisees

45

give Jesus about King Herod. Jesus knows this "fox" cannot touch him because a prophet cannot die outside Jerusalem (13.31-33). In the passion story only Luke includes the scene about Herod. Jesus refused even to speak to that puppet.

COST OF DISCIPLESHIP

Please read: Luke 14.25-33

During the journey to Jerusalem Luke pictures big crowds following Jesus. He turns and addresses them in some of the strongest New Testament words about the conditions for being his disciples. Would-be followers of Jesus must "hate" every member of their families including parents and wives—even their own lives—to be his disciples. The role is like building a tower. Unless deep foundations are laid, it will collapse.

This stress on the total and absolute supremacy of Jesus over every other choice reveals Luke's teaching on the coming of Jesus. It is God's apocalyptic intervention in the world. It is the beginning of the final age. Such a time allows no compromise.

No wonder the disciples cry out, "Increase our faith." Jesus says they need faith only the size of a mustard seed. Its built-in dynamism will effect marvels (17.5-6). This saying of Jesus is a warning against looking on God's gifts as our own accomplishment—a real danger for zealous disciples. The power of faith becomes so much a part of them that they are tempted to think of it as a personal accomplishment.

The tendency to place too much reliance on personal ability would be particularly common for Luke's audience. He wrote for self-reliant Greeks skilled in practical wisdom. They could easily think that their insight created the future.

Against this attitude Luke retains the saying of Jesus, " The kingdom of God does not come with observation," that is, in a way that is the subject of human investigation (17.20). Otherwise God would be subject to human control. Believers freely move beyond earthly preoccupations because of the power of Christ's imminent presence.

The effect of his resurrection and glorification is already being felt upon the community. It is the lordship of Jesus that brings believers to salvation. Luke stresses this power because the delay of the Lord's return was troubling members of the Church. They were disappointed at the long wait.

Luke shows that the risen Jesus is already present. He shows this by bringing part of the material from Jesus' last will and testament into the advice he gives his disciples on their way to Jerusalem (17.22-37). What people do each day has a direct bearing on their final judgment. The punishments of God at the time of Noah and Lot serve as illustrations.

Daily life since the coming of Jesus has an apocalyptic level. The end time is not "out there" in some distant place. It is the wider reality into which Jesus has brought us through his death and resurrection. All humanity is involved.

By accepting the lordship of Jesus and the kingdom he offers, believers have also begun the "ascension" to the heavenly city. The Son of Man who suffered in lowliness on Calvary will come back to take his followers with him into glory.

JESUS REACHES OUT TO THE ALIENATED

Please read: Luke 6.20-36

The majority of converts from paganism to the Christian religion were from lower classes. Long before Luke, Paul reminded the Corinthians that not many of them were powerful or of noble lineage (1 Cor 1.26). Luke pictures Jesus as spending much of his time with the alienated. In his opening address at Nazareth Jesus quotes from the prophet Isaiah. The Spirit of the Lord sent him to preach the good news to the poor (4.18).

47

After choosing his disciples Jesus gives an important sermon. We can take this address as performing a function similar to Matthew's Sermon on the Mount. The switch in geographical location is symbolic. Jesus reserves the mountain to speak to God. To the people he talks on the plain.

Jesus begins by invoking a blessing on "you poor—for yours is the kingdom of God" (6.20). His sermon is not to the poor as an abstract concept but to the crowd before him as materially powerless. They are blessed in God's plan because they have no human resources to bring them success in this life. In turning to God they receive the freedom of his kingdom.

Jesus warns that material goods attract to themselves. They absorb human talent and leave persons without the energy needed to work for building up God's reign.

Jesus declares other groups of alienated people as blessed also. They are considered weak and wretched by this world's standards: the hungry, the mourners, the despised (6.21-22). But their heavenly Father is preparing a better destiny for them. The coming of Jesus has turned human standards upside down. He warns the rich, the sated, the laughing, the honored among men. They can too easily put their trust in this age.

On the contrary, Jesus celebrates a foolhardy generosity in dealing with others. His followers must not measure by human standards like self-preservation, ambition or security. Not only are they to accept rejection by the powers that be of this world but they are to reach out in love toward their enemies, lend without expecting a return. In this way believers imitate God who showers blessings on the ungrateful and evil.

The ideal Jesus offers is to be "compassionate as your heavenly Father is compassionate" (6.36). Jesus displayed this ideal by going out to his enemies and eating with them. By this openness he invited them to embrace the salvation God wishes to give to all his children.

48

RADICAL DEMANDS OF JESUS

As a hero dedicated to God's work the earthly Jesus makes radical demands on his followers. He lived in austere poverty. He had "nowhere to lay his head" (9.58). Luke pictures Jesus as often inviting his followers to live in the same way.

The first ones Jesus invited to follow him were fishermen. This was a profitable profession at the Lake of Galilee. When Jesus called Simon Peter, James, and John, they left all things to follow him (5.11). The same demand is met by the tax collector Levi (5.28).

Later Jesus sent out seventy-two disciples to prepare cities for his coming. He ordered them not to carry either "money bag" or "beggar's bag" (10.4). The latter was standard equipment for itinerant Cynic preachers of that time. In other words, his disciples were not to enrich themselves through their service of the good news. On the contrary, unless one "sells all he possesses, he cannot be my disciple" (14.33).

Jesus demands daily asceticism of his followers. They must take up the cross "every day and follow Jesus" (9.23). Most modern readers find such a regime excessive—not to mention impractical.

Moreover, even Jesus is not pictured as following such a regime. The Jews complained that Jesus did not observe the ascetical practices they identified with religious reformers. They contrasted him with John the Baptizer and called him "glutton and drunkard" (7.34). And Luke shows that Jesus dined with leading Pharisees (7.36; 14.1).

It is Luke also who indicates that the faithful women disciples of Jesus "administered to him and his disciples out of their possessions" (8.3). So they had not sold everything!

How then are we to understand these radical demands of Jesus? What he is teaching by these severe sayings is that his followers cannot live a shallow form of existence. They must transcend the standards of this world with its superficial preoccupations and selfish lifestyle.

To live on a material level is to place one's trust in things that are passing and unable to save. It is to be like the rich fool who tried to provide for his future by building bigger barns. He said to his soul, "Eat, drink and be merry!" But God said to him, "Fool, this night your soul is demanded." And Jesus drew a lesson for all. "This is everyone who stores up treasures for himself and is not rich toward God" (13.19-21).

JESUS CALLS TO CONFIDENCE

Please read: Luke 12.22-34

Luke shows less interest in the miracles of Jesus than in his personal relationships with a wide variety of people. In all of his dealings Jesus incarnates the compassionate love of his Father to bring peace.

To have divine peace is to be rich toward God—rich in trust and in hope. This is the good that Luke holds out to his readers. In reality the great demands that Jesus makes are not primarily negative or restrictive. Far from being impossible they liberate believers from the slavery of this world.

As a result the overall tone of Luke's Gospel is positive. It is good news—full of joy and encouragement. The cross frees followers of Jesus from slavery to this material world. It places them under the guidance of the Holy Spirit, who led the earthly Jesus.

No human force can win eternal life. True wisdom then is to trust in God as Jesus did. Luke preserves a discourse on confidence that Jesus gave in response to a man asking him to make his brother share their inheritance. This sermon is a good example of the approach Jesus urges toward material concerns.

Jesus raises the questioner's horizons to a higher plane. Only in seeing reality from a spiritual point of view can we hope to achieve an integration of all human values in God's plan. Believers acquire this vision best by prayer.

No wonder Luke puts so much emphasis on prayer in his Gospel—both in the ministry of Jesus and in the life of believers. Jesus turns to prayer as part of every major event in his life, such as his baptism, his transfiguration and his choice of his apostles.

The intensity of his prayer life impressed his disciples. One morning after Jesus spent the whole night praying, they came to him and asked how to pray. Jesus responded by giving the shorter and direct Lukan version of the Lord's Prayer (11.2-4).

For Luke one of the most important forms of prayer is listening to the word of God. This is what the mother of Jesus did. This is the "better part" that the other Mary, sister of Martha and friend of Jesus, chose (10.38-42).

Prayer and confidence in God lead to the spiritual childhood Jesus recommends (18.17). The parable of the widow and the wicked judge illustrates that believers "must always pray and never grow weary" (18.1). We are to engage in the experience of prayer "boldly," confident that this approach opens all doors to the divine presence. The heavenly Father will not refuse a Holy Spirit to those who beg him (11.8-13).

SUGGESTIONS FOR REFLECTION

1. Who were the Hellenes and why did Luke write for them? Why was his approach to the Gospel different from that of Matthew and Mark? How did hero-lore and kingship tracts affect Luke's style? How were his writings about Jesus different from the writings about other popular heroes of the Greek culture? What other source did Luke and Matthew both use?

2. As you recall Luke's Gospel, give an instance in which a believer was liberated by Jesus. Mention an occasion in which a believer was enslaved by Jesus and his message. What kind of Jesus was Luke interested in depicting?

3. How does the infancy narrative build up the idea that Jesus is Lord?

4. Luke's Gospel is sometimes thought of as the Gospel of the Holy Spirit. Give some examples to illustrate this thought.

5. What is the meaning of "slave" implied in Luke's use by Our Lady and by Paul? Is this symbolic word helpful today to Americans? How meaningful is it for you personally?

6. Some people think miracles were performed to create faith in the witnesses. At times the miracles were performed to reward the faith of the person needing a cure. Which approach to faith did Luke emphasize—faith as a result of God's action, or faith as a prerequisite to God's saving action?

7. What technique does Luke use to highlight the theological meaning of Jesus' journey up to Jerusalem? What bearing does this journey to Jerusalem have on the life of a disciple today? How do the Sunday Gospel readings help in this?

8. Luke depicts the life of discipleship as:
—believing in Jesus radically,
—loving him even more intensely than one's family,
—planning thoroughly, but
—leaning totally on his gifts rather than trusting in one's personal ability, etc.
To what extent do you observe these characteristics in Christian disciples today? How does your life fit the description?

9. For Luke, "the end time is not 'out there' in some distant place." How is the end already here and now?

10. As you look at "the poor" today do you class yourself among them? Why does Jesus consider the poor, the alienated, and persecuted persons as truly rich? Is this a trend in current thinking?

11. Jesus seems to condemn measuring success by ambition, security, and self-preservation. What life plan would Jesus give today's graduates at their commencement exercises?

12. The kind of trust in God that Luke shows Jesus as recommending requires a wholly spiritual vision about the values of life. How is such a spiritual vision reached? Is it one of your personal and realistic life values? You can gauge what you truly value by noting how much time you spend with it each day, in a week. How long is it since you asked the heavenly Father for the gift of the Holy Spirit?

CHAPTER V

MATTHEW, THE PREACHER'S GUIDE

A person who reads Mark's Gospel first and then turns to that of Matthew encounters both similarities and differences. The two narrate some scenes from the ministry of Jesus in almost exactly the same terms. Enough of these agreements occur to affirm a close relationship.

At the same time, however, Matthew contains large segments with no parallel in Mark. The creation of Gospel as a literary genre did not put an end to internal development within this type of literature. Quite the contrary.

Once a continuous Gospel narrative was created, it was used in liturgy year after year. The selections stimulated questions about the life and teaching of Jesus. Such questions came from community interests. Individual evangelists responded to these interests according to their own purposes.

MATTHEW'S AUDIENCE

Please read: Matthew 1.18–2.23

Groups of Christians converted from Judaism began to search through their Hebrew Scriptures to figure out why Jesus acted the way he did. Why did God's chosen people reject their Messiah? Features of Matthew's Gospel point to its origin in such a group.

One of its most striking characteristics is a series of ten biblical quotations scattered throughout the work. These have a series of distinctive features that separate them from other uses of the Old Testament:

(1) they are all editorial comments by Matthew himself. In other words, they do not occur on the lips of Jesus or of any other character in the story.

(2) they link some event of the life of Jesus to a specific passage in Jewish Scriptures. The quotation may be an exact translation of the Hebrew Bible. Or it may be based on the existing Greek translation. Or it may be a paraphrase. The form is chosen to fit the event in Jesus' life.

(3) they reflect the theology of Matthew. He asks readers to see the biblical texts through his eyes. He is making a careful effort to use the Old Testament to enrich Christian faith. To do so Matthew adopts the current rabbinical method of interpreting passages. Rabbis at the time of Matthew were using a great variety of literary devices (puns, plays on words, etymologies) and logical conceits to make Scripture speak to the contemporary scene. Matthew's use of this method indicates he writes for believers acquainted with the unity of salvation history.

(4) these quotations must be read in that framework before they can speak to today's readers. For example, when Joseph brings Jesus back from Egypt, he finds that Herod's son is ruling in Judea. So Joseph settles in Nazareth "so that what was spoken by the prophets might be fulfilled—he shall be called a Nazorean" (2.23).

Matthew and his intended audience knew well that the town of Nazareth is never mentioned in the Old Testament. What then does the quotation mean? It is obviously a play on words.

Such a method implies a rabbinical school somewhere in the tradition of Matthew. Unfortunately it seems impossible to determine which of two or three Hebrew words Matthew had in mind. It could be the "shoot" of David or the "Nazirite" vow. In any case, this procedure is the fruit of active faith. It sets the tone for how this Gospel is to be read.

EMERGENCE OF THE TRUE ISRAEL

Please read: Matthew 8.1-17

The Bible was important for Matthew. He saw it pointing to the mission of Jesus who came to bring every part of it to completion. This God-given task brought Jesus into tension with the Mosaic community of his day.

This tension dominates the unfolding of Matthew's Gospel. He employs three literary techniques to maintain this tension throughout the whole length of his writing. They are:

(1) schematizing. Matthew reduces narratives to general schemas by eliminating as many details as possible. Scenes thus become universal models of conduct.

(2) systematizing. Matthew groups common themes together. Above all, he gathers his teaching materials into comprehensive sermons to give an overall picture of what Jesus commands. This is true especially for the Sermon on the Mount and the parable discourse. Both are treated below. Another example is the mission discourse (10.5-42). That sermon serves as a guide for earlier Christian missionary preachers.

(3) synthesizing. Matthew is careful to offer a clear picture of the Christian ideals. He provides editorial guidance for his readers. He eliminates confusing expressions and assists his readers to interpret the message of Jesus.

These carefully elaborated literary techniques serve Matthew's theological purpose. In one sense we can say that his goal is to show the Church as the true Israel. It is the perfection toward which the law and the prophets were pointing.

Every event in the life of Jesus as recorded in Matthew in some way serves as a step in the setting up of the Church. Jesus came to found the kingdom of the heavens. What he left behind was a community of believers, the Church. As a result, trust in the Church is trust in Jesus. That is where he exercises his lordship in the world.

To achieve this direction Matthew modifies the shaping principle of Gospel with long sections of teaching material. His Gospel provides preachers in the new Israel with developed presentations on which to base their sermons.

THE SERMON ON THE MOUNT

Please read: Matthew 5.1—7.29

This is a sermon for the religious and moral guidance of the Church as the true Israel.

Like the other evangelists, Matthew writes for members of the Christian community who had not seen Jesus. As a teacher he organizes instructional material from his tradition into an easy-to-use form. During Jesus' life on earth he gave his wisdom slowly in a piecemeal fashion to bewildered followers. Matthew does not try to recapture this growing process. He organizes and synthesizes instructions of the Master into a final ready-to-use presentation.

Matthew's most famous example of this process occurs near the opening of the Lord's public life. Matthew places the Sermon on the Mount there. It is a comprehensive overview of Christian morality as fulfilling the law of Moses.

Jesus starts with a set of beatitudes, a Hebrew form of blessing. The approach is important. It sets the tone for the new law. He is not giving a set of limit commands aimed primarily to keep his followers from evil.

The new law is a positive force. Jesus sets believers' hearts in motion toward fulfilling God's loving will to save. Matthew calls it "justice" (5.6). The purpose of Jesus' coming is not to oppose the law God gave to the Jews but rather to achieve its goal.

Jesus describes this fuller justice of God in the form of six contrasts between the lesser demands of the law of Moses and his own commands. God is no longer satisfied to have his children refrain from evil. They must direct their lives and talents toward doing God's will in every area of life.

Christian morality means great self-control. It respects the neighbor's physical life, marriage, good name and property. In his Sermon on the Mount Jesus proclaims that his Father asks for perfect honesty in speech, complete forgiveness from the heart and creative love of enemies. In a word Christians are to imitate the perfection of their heavenly Father (5.21-48).

This fuller identification with God expresses itself in a purification of the three ascetical practices encouraged by the law of Moses. These are called almsgiving, prayer and fasting (6.2-18). These terms are meant to be understood in the broadest sense. They synthesize the whole range of responsible conduct toward the neighbor, God and self.

The Sermon on the Mount closes with final admonitions to put these commands of Jesus into action. It is not enough for believers to talk. They are called to build up a spiritual life by solid deeds (7.21-27).

PARABLES OF THE KINGDOM

Please read: Matthew 13.1-52

In the very center of his Gospel Matthew collects seven key parables about the kingdom or reign of God.

This symbol of God's powerful presence in Jesus is the heart of his revelation. This divine presence is mysterious and paradoxical. It is already at work calling us to obedient faith. But it is not yet manifest in all its glory.

Jesus spoke of God's activity as king in parables because this form of expression reflected his experience of God's saving will. God cannot be boxed into human concepts. He overturns all obstacles blocking the completion of his plan. Jesus saw human destiny in terms of a world-shaping drama that embraced all creation. It was moving to fulfillment in himself.

The Father casts his saving net wide to engulf all creatures. This vision of Jesus about how much God wanted to save all mankind expressed itself in his parables, especially those of the kingdom. God does not work according to human rules. The kingdom is like a pearl valuable beyond the wildest imagination of the sophisticated dealer in precious stones. God's presence is joy beyond compare.

Jesus' experience generated parables—metaphors that carry us beyond literal language. Matthew transmits the parables of Jesus only in an extremely condensed version. He reduces them to the barest outline of:

revelation—some aspect of the saving power of God. No one of them says everything, but each offers an aspect of the mystery of the kingdom.

revolution—the overthrowing of all previous limited visions about God. Parables open up new possibilities and challenges.

resolution—the call to radical choice. To enter the kingdom we must leave behind the old world and its selfish values.

THE CENTRAL ROLE OF ST. PETER

Please read: Matthew 16.13–17.27

Following the parable discourse, Matthew devotes special attention to St. Peter. As author of the Church Gospel, Matthew grounds all Church authority in the deliberate will of Jesus to continue his mission through chosen followers.

After the multiplication of the loaves, Jesus sent his disciples away so he could pray alone. During the night their boat was battered by winds. Jesus walked over the sea toward them. When they saw him, they thought they saw a ghost. But Jesus reassured them. Peter wanted to test the situation and asked permission to come. Jesus invited him and Peter began to walk confidently. Then his faith failed. Jesus reached out to support him with the words "one of little faith." This rescue prompted all in the boat to worship Jesus as Son of God (14.33).

Matthew uses this scene to prepare for Peter's great confession of faith at Caesarea Philippi. Jesus took his disciples into pagan territory to find out how he was being received. After other disciples reported their opinions, Peter spoke for all the disciples. He confessed Jesus as "the Christ, the Son of the living God" (16.16).

Jesus proclaims this as an act of faith possible only as a divine gift. The Father himself revealed this to Peter. But gift brings responsibility. Peter's role from now on will be to teach and guide the Church. In recognition of this honor Jesus officially assigns the name "rock" to him.

This new role does not immediately eliminate Peter's weakness or ambition. When Jesus goes on to predict that he must suffer and be put to death, Peter objects. Jesus should put such ideas out of his mind. Jesus angrily addresses Peter as "Satan," the Adversary. Peter belongs in the same class as the devil who tried earlier to divert Jesus from his God-given mission.

Peter also plays a prominent part in the transfiguration of Jesus. Overwhelmed by the appearance of Moses and Elijah and by the glory shining in the face of Jesus, Peter wanted to erect a shrine. The Lord rejects the offer and tells his disciples not to speak of the event until he is risen from the dead.

INSTRUCTIONS FOR CHURCH MEMBERS

Please read: Matthew 18.1-35

The most striking feature of Matthew's Gospel is the way he presents all actions of the earthly Jesus as steps to founding the Church. And so a crucial element of his narration is to show Jesus instructing his disciples as founding members of the true Israel.

In keeping with his practice of synthesizing, Matthew groups these instructions into a long discourse. A question put by a disciple about who will have the most important post in the kingdom provides the occasion. Jesus answers by illustrating the nature of authority in his Church.

In no way are his disciples to imitate the style of contemporary pagan rulers. On the contrary, Christian leaders must adopt the simplicity of little children. That means putting aside all personal ambition and relying totally upon the power at work in the kingdom. Only when they recognize that they cannot establish the kingdom of God by human wisdom or skill are believers able to accept it as a grace.

In particular, Christian leaders must be at the service of all just as Jesus was. He so identified with the weak that the leaders of his Church cannot continue his mission without being totally available to them.

In graphic language Jesus points out the responsibility of Church members to protect the weak and vulnerable from sin. The heavenly Father is the true Shepherd who does not want to lose any of his flock. Just as Jesus is willing to go to any length to guide the Father's children to salvation, so members of his Church are to be available to all in need.

In this compelling sermon Matthew lays down principles for mutual concern and reconciliation. Offended members are to seek out their offender to restore unity. Only if individual efforts prove unsuccessful is a wider circle of witnesses to be summoned. As a last resort, "Tell the Church" (18.17). The whole community maintains discipline and encourages unity in the face of outside misunderstanding and repression.

A careful reading of this discourse indicates that Matthew has the needs of his own community in mind in these questions. He is fostering the ministry of reconciliation in a divided community. Peter's question about how often Christians are to forgive an erring member brings an unexpected call to generosity—not seven but seventy-seven times. This unbounded spirit of generosity is a pale reflection of God's infinite compassion.

Jesus illustrates forgiveness in the parable of the rich property owner. He forgives at the mere display of profound need. Yet his pardon does not endure when his servant shows himself unresponsive to the needs of others. Readers hear an echo of the Lord's Prayer—forgive us as we forgive.

THE CALL TO WATCHFULNESS

Please read: Matthew 24.1–25.46

Before entering into his passion Jesus addresses his last will and testament to his disciples. He wants them to view what is happening now in terms of the overarching plan of God.

After driving the money changers from the temple Jesus must leave Jerusalem at night to seek a safe place to sleep. His disciples remark about the beauty of the temple then being rebuilt according to the grandiose plan of Herod. Jesus shocks them by saying that it will be destroyed completely.

Their request for an explanation provides Matthew with the occasion for Jesus to elaborate on the certainty of his parousia. This is the glorious coming of the Son of Man (see Mt 24.3, 27, 37, 39). This mysterious apocalyptic sermon exists in different versions in the Gospels of Mark and Luke.

An apocalyptic sermon cannot be analyzed logically. It is to be understood as a symbolic portrayal of the cosmic struggle facing the Church in this world. The key to salvation is trust in God. "He who perseveres unto the end will be saved" (24.13) is a phrase Matthew repeats from the mission discourse (10.22).

WAITING IN HOPE

Matthew presents the foresight of Jesus in more hopeful terms than does Mark. He does not play down the cosmic dimensions of the struggle. Yet the word of God will support believers and prevail over enemies. So he puts more emphasis on responding to Jesus with confidence. How?

His Gospel does not move directly from the apocalyptic sermon to the Last Supper. Instead Matthew inserts three parables of watchfulness. He reminds us we do not know when the Son of Man will return as judge.

(1) The first is the parable of the wicked servant who thinks that his master will not return without warning. So he is caught maltreating his fellow servants (24.45-51).

(2) Then comes the last of the parables of the kingdom, the story of the ten virgins. The five foolish ones do not keep attentive for the bridegroom. They fall asleep and lose out on the wedding (25.1-13).

(3) Finally comes the parable of the talents. It too offers encouragement to Christians to use God's gifts intelligently (25.14-30).

Matthew brings these pleas for watchfulness to a glorious close in the majestic vision of final judgment. In context, this is a call to live out of strong faith in the power of the good news. The response of faith does not remain idle but devotes all of its energy to the service of the Lord in his little ones.

THE GREAT COMMISSION

Please read: Matthew 28.16-20

In a sense the whole Gospel of Matthew leads up to its final scene—the great commission. He has been preparing his readers for it by emphasizing the teaching authority of Jesus and by the scenes featuring the activity of his disciples.

The infancy narrative revealed that Jesus should be called Immanuel, "God with us." After the resurrection, Jesus comes back to his disciples to teach how this is destined to be fulfilled. He will no longer be present to the world in visible bodily form. From now on Jesus remains in the world through a new kind of presence—the Church.

The Gospel pictures the disciples as believing in the risen Jesus even before they see him. They recognize him when he manifests himself in Galilee and bow down in homage. Jesus' address to them consists of three parts:

(1) a revelation. "All authority in heaven and on earth has been given to me." Jesus spent his whole life exercising his authority, as God's Son, to teach and heal—even to forgive sin. The full scope of that authority was not revealed until after the resurrection.

Jesus joins his Father as Lord of the universe. He is able to relate to creatures in a transforming way without being limited by time or space. This is his mysterious power as Savior. Now he reveals how he exercises it.

64

(2) a commission. Jesus identifies his Church fully with his saving mission. Just as he taught the Jews of his age, so his followers are to go forth to teach the whole human race. The ones who accept him celebrate their allegiance publicly in the sacrament of baptism.

Baptism incorporates believers into the life of Father, Son and Holy Spirit. Since the Holy Spirit had not yet been poured out upon the Church in Matthew's Gospel, this scene is to be understood as telescoping the period leading to a full understanding of the Trinity. Such knowledge was acquired by the Church's experience of his indwelling.

(3) a promise. Matthew ends his Gospel with an allusion to why the angel said Jesus was to be called Immanuel. He works in the world in and through his Church. Loyalty to the Church is loyalty to Jesus.

Those who enter the community of believers enjoy the fruits of his abiding presence. This new presence of Jesus through his Spirit is even more real and powerful than his earthly one. Through his Church Jesus fulfills the law and the prophets and prevails over the gates of the underworld.

SUGGESTIONS FOR REFLECTION

1. Read Matthew 1.18 through 2.23, and find distinctive passages that show that his audience must have been Jewish.

2. To emphasize his theological goal Matthew used the techniques of schematizing, systematizing, and synthesizing. What was his goal? How does he distinguish the Church from the kingdom?

3. Matthew synthesizes the positive new law in the Eight Beatitudes. Read again the Ten Commandments and the Eight Beati-

tudes (Mt 5.1-11) to notice the difference in tone, spirit, and attitudes preached by each.

4. The law of Moses had recommended almsgiving, prayer, and fasting. How do the Eight Beatitudes extend the understanding of each of these practices?

5. For Matthew, what is the kingdom? Why are parables the best way to describe its mystery? Which parable of the kingdom do you prefer? What revolution or resolution does it suggest to you?

6. Read each of the parables of the kingdom in Chapter 13. Note what vision-change or value-change each is advocating. Compose a present-day parable of the kingdom for your family.

7. If Matthew is known for his Gospel of the Church, why did he place the stories about Peter so close to the parables of the kingdom?

8. According to Matthew's Gospel, Jesus is teaching that:
   a) We cannot build the Church or the kingdom on human wisdom and skill alone.
   b) We must model authority in the Church on the simplicity of a child, the service of a servant, and the care of a shepherd.
   c) When injustice occurs we are to forgive the offender without limit.
Do you think Jesus meant these literally? Explain why they are or are not realistic guidelines for building a community where God's presence is seen? Are they realistic guidelines for the Church today?

9. In Chapter 24 how does Matthew represent the final struggle between the reign of God and the reign of evil? What response does Jesus hope to evoke?

10. How has the Church tangibly responded through the centuries to the discourse of Matthew 25.31-46? How are you responding to it in your life call?

11. "And know that I am with you always. . . " (Mt 28.20) How can this be true even into our times? How can we tell that this chapter must have been written some years after the events and speeches recorded?

CHAPTER VI

PARABLES REVEAL THE KINGDOM

As I said in Chapter I, the Gospels are primarily revelations. And revelation belongs to the realm of religious language. Its purpose is not to inform of some facts about a God "out there." Rather revelation is God's making himself available to humans in the risen Jesus as final destiny of every person.

How deeply Jesus was aware of that mystery in his human consciousness during his life on earth is not clear from the Gospels. Yet certainly Jesus was vividly aware that God was his Father. He knew God was acting within him and through him to exercise a new saving power and presence on earth.

In the synoptic Gospels that presence is often called "the kingdom of God," or "kingdom of the heavens" in Matthew. Here Matthew adopts the current Jewish custom of referring to God in substitute terms. Heaven stands for God.

The synoptic Gospels picture Jesus as offering the gift of the kingdom by means of parables. They use the term parable 48 times (17 in Mt; 13 in Mk; 18 in Lk).

The word describes a wide variety of expressions we do not ordinarily call parables in English. It covers the spectrum from short proverbs to metaphors to full-length illustrations. For example, Luke uses it for the sentence, "Physician, heal yourself" (4.23) and "The blind can't lead the blind, can they?" (6.39). New Testament commentators call many comparisons that are not explicitly named parables by this term.

This flexibility in the term must be kept in mind when dealing with their use by Jesus. Basically a parable is a metaphor or comparison. The Greek word means "thrown along side." It is always a figurative use of language. Hence, it includes meanings deeper than the literal use of its words.

WHY JESUS SPOKE IN PARABLES

Please read: Mark 4.1-34

For readers of the Gospels the question naturally arises why Jesus chose this literary form. Why did he make it the usual mode for revelation in speech?

This question had arisen in the early Church. What still appears striking today is that the Gospels answered it in several ways. They preserved the variety of opinions existing in the early Church. Instead of choosing one answer, the evangelists incorporated current opinions side by side.

This tells us, of course, that the question has many answers. We can go further. It tells us that none of these answers is the total reason why Jesus spoke in parables. The reasons given grew out of reflection by early believers on the impact of Jesus' revelation.

This reflection is preserved in the paradoxical answers Jesus gave for his method. It comes after the parable of the sower. In all three synoptic Gospels the disciples ask why he speaks to the crowds in parables.

His answer always links parables to outsiders. Jesus strangely says that he does not speak to the disciples in parables. He uses parables for those who do not accept the mystery of the kingdom. This answer is paradoxical because Jesus openly said he came to reveal the kingdom and to teach. In fact, Mark opens the discourse with the comment that Jesus "started to teach them many things in parables" (Mk 4.2).

69

In his version of the parable discourse Matthew adds one of his "fulfillment" quotes. Jesus taught in parables to fulfill the prophetic passage that he would proclaim things hidden since the foundation of the world (Mt 13.35, citing Ps 78.2).

Why this conflict? Because of a change of emphasis in the course of time. The observation that the crowds did not understand the mystery of the kingdom refers to the actual result of Jesus' teaching at the time the Gospels were written. The evangelists incorporated the experience of Christian communities during the generation following the resurrection.

The majority of the Jewish people did not respond to the preaching of the apostles. So they are seen as identifying themselves with the negative response their ancestors gave the prophets. The evangelists saw this as another aspect of Scripture being fulfilled.

At the same time the writers of the Gospels indicate this rejection of Jesus was not what Jesus wanted. He faithfully carried out his mission to reveal God's saving love. Parables played an important part in that mission.

PARABLES AS REVELATION

Early Christians found it hard to understand the rejection of Jesus by his own. It almost seemed that God's plan had failed! But their faith could not accept that solution. This tension forced them to wonder why Jesus chose parables as the major method of revealing by word.

Parables were not a substitute for some superior method. Jesus did not choose them as a way of patronizing ignorant peasants. Those who came to hear him were religious people well acquainted with the law of Moses and Jewish Scriptures.

Jesus appreciated this and invited them to move closer to the goals of God's will than the law of Moses could take them.

70

His mission was to communicate his own experience of his Father's power and love working in him. What Jesus knew through his total and prayerful submission to God's Spirit, he wanted to share with them.

His role was not that of a human teacher stimulating native intelligence to master some material. Jesus' task was of a different nature. It was to uncover divine truth and invite people to shape their lives by his empowered vision. For this unique mission the parables were the appropriate literary vehicle.

Parables operate as mini-dramas. Their story conveys some insight about an aspect of God's kingdom as a call to new life and salvation. In a profound sense we can say that Jesus did not choose parables. They chose him! So much was he caught up in the divine mystery.

These images sprang from his sharp powers of observation and were totally at the disposal of his religious commitment. He was able to fill images familiar to his audience with divine insight. All creation spoke to him of the kingdom—the nets used by Galilean fishermen, the kneading of bread, the hard lot of day laborers, the ambition of the rich, a fig tree.

Jesus was so in tune with the power of God that he saw the different aspects of the kingdom of God mirrored in events of everyday life. His parables were figurative expressions of how these events point beyond this world.

Note that Jesus compared the kingdom to the whole activity taking place, not to static elements. Parables are always stories that open up action within the kingdom. They reveal spiritual truth that invites faith and conversion. Every parable, as a call to discipleship, becomes meaningful only by producing a change of heart.

The ability of these dramas to express his religious depth made them appropriate for use by Jesus. God involves himself with humans by offering a share in his life as their ultimate goal and destiny. Through his parables Jesus communicated this new world to his hearers. Hence the challenge.

To enter this new world his hearers had to leave their old one behind. Many in his audience refused to do so. For them the parables became condemnation instead of new life. Even the little they had would be taken away (Mt 25.29).

PARABLES AS MIRACLES IN WORDS

Please read: Luke 18.9-14

How did this dramatization of revelation's call to conversion and new life operate? It functioned as religious language. Jesus did not relate facts about the kingdom but produced decisions for it. Parables enlightened and empowered hearers to accept the values and demands of the kingdom.

In a real sense they operated as miracles in words because they brought hearers to entrust their destiny to God. By his parables Jesus inspired the trust and vision that animated his own life. They deepened the faith and wisdom of receptive hearts to acknowledge the truth and to choose it.

For those willing to admit their need for the kingdom and its power, the parables brought healing from alienation. They gave a sense of wholeness to life. The hope communicated in parable brought hearers to identify with the final destiny Jesus proclaimed.

He communicated the sense of being in touch with satisfying reality. And his parables gave an inkling of the possibilities available to those who followed and imitated him. He uprooted listeners from the self-centered love that destroys life. To choose to lose one's life for the kingdom is a miracle of healing and hope.

That kind of conversion embraces the plan of God as making sense out of the ambiguities of human life. So parables make

72

believers able and willing to enlist in the drama of salvation lovingly and hopefully. In their faith decision followers of Jesus become truly human. For they allow God to be their God and to rule their destiny.

THE PARABLE OF THE SOWER

Please read: Matthew 13.1-23

Each of the three synoptic Gospels has a special parable discourse. Matthew greatly extends his in accord with his method of expanding the teaching of Jesus and grouping his material in a systematic way (Mt 13.1-52). Luke, on the contrary, sharply curtails his discourse, in keeping with his method of short groups of similar material (Lk 8.4-18).

Yet the three evangelists all begin this section with the parable of the sower and all include an explanation of it. To have an explanation of a parable is rare. But what is more striking is that this explanation does not correspond exactly to the parable. It deals with the fate of the seeds sown rather than with the sower.

The uniformity of the three accounts indicates that this parable played a significant role in early Christian preaching. Evidently this explanation grew up during the period when preachers applied the parable to actual fruits of evangelization by the apostles.

Is it possible to go back beyond the resurrection and grasp the parable of the sower in the context of the earthly life of Jesus?

To do this we have to pay close attention to the words of the parable itself and less attention to the setting. I already pointed out above that the question about teaching in parables refers to divisions arising after the resurrection. It was directed to the refusal of many to accept the mystery of the kingdom and join the Christian community.

An analysis of the parable itself indicates it is a parable about understanding parables. Jesus dramatizes the mystery of God's word. The story level is easy to grasp. Jesus draws details from a scene of planting by scattering the seed, as was customary in Palestine—a scene familiar to his readers, if not to us.

But many possibilities open up on a deeper level. Jesus is not repeating commonplace information about matters his hearers already know. The message of the parable lies on the metaphorical level of the fate of the word of God.

To be more specific, Jesus speaks of the word of God that he as Son is making available. The parable tells about tensions revelation creates in every call to conversion. There are many ways of not hearing and not responding.

Some people never understand the demands of conversion. They do not let the kingdom receive a hearing. For them conversion is never considered. Others put limits on their will to hear. Their shallow spirit is incapable of opening to the richness of the word. When it begins to sprout they cannot commit themselves to nourish it.

Others are capable and competent but also uncommitted to the challenge of the word of God. They can see its beauty but they have many other attractions in life. So they compromise. And by their lack of surrender to its demands they choke the word in their lives. This is another way of not hearing.

THE DEMANDS OF THE WORD OF GOD

Only those coming to parables with depths of personal faith provide adequate soil for the word to grow. For when God's word finds a reception, it becomes ever more demanding. It wants to take possession of the whole person.

To become a disciple of Jesus one must give all. The parable of the sower is another illustration of the truth that he who loses his life for Jesus and for the Gospel finds it.

In some way all parables lead hearers to embrace that truth. We do not hear them until they evoke that decision. The intimate exchange between seed and soil serves as appropriate symbol of the nature of every parable as a religious dialogue. It is carried on not on the surface of the soul but only in total obedience to God's all-embracing claims.

God makes these claims in a whole spectrum of insights. And their implications cover the whole range of human response. In the preaching of Jesus the image of kingdom of God serves as symbol for both demand and possibility implicit in a full response of faith.

The drama of the sower is not called a parable of the kingdom but it sheds light on what is implied in accepting it. On the one hand, it means living in an end-time horizon in carrying out one's activities. Human destiny is not measured by goals of human making but by a share in God's eternal plan.

On the other hand, the kingdom Jesus proclaims demands mature personal responsibility. The choice is made by being converted to its values every day. Matthew's Gospel stresses that aspect frequently. So we turn to his grouping of the parables of the kingdom.

PARABLES OF THE KINGDOM IN MATTHEW

Please read: Matthew 13.24-49

The related group of expressions about "the kingdom (reign) of God (heaven, Father, Son)" appears in the synoptic Gospels eighty-six times. These phrases never appear in the Hebrew Bible even though the idea of God as king was common among Jews. Its arrival is a summary of the revelation of Jesus.

The kingdom was a reality beyond ordinary comprehension and accomplishment by mortals. In a word, a mystery. Parables pointed to this mystery and invited hearers to celebrate it by faith response.

At times Christians identify kingdom with Church. The two
are related but not identical. Matthew, the author of the Church
Gospel, gives the most parables about the kingdom—ten in all.
He groups seven of them in the very center of his Gospel in his
third great discourse. Up to that point Matthew does not record
any parables of Jesus.

By bringing a whole series of these parables together Matthew
is able to synthesize what Jesus taught over a long period of
time. This method places the kingdom of God in prominence
and invites his readers to enter the new age. It also stresses the
paradoxes involved in this choice.

The goal of these parables is not to convey information about
aspects of the kingdom or to give technical knowledge or theo-
retical concepts. Readers are able to enter because the kingdom
invites them. The grace and power of God chooses and attracts
believers like the pearl of great price. It makes all sacrifices
worthwhile (Mt 13.45-46).

In other words, these parables are speech events granting to believers the keys to enter the kingdom. They translate the universal saving mission of Jesus into concrete choices. To hear is
to experience the power of Jesus at work like the leaven transforming one's world (Mt 13.33).

Jesus saw that all would not accept the kingdom of God. At
times the dragnet of his preaching caught very few fish and even
some of these had to be let go.

These parables show that for Jesus the kingdom was a reality.
It was already bursting upon him and imposing his mission.
After his death the kingdom was identified with Jesus himself.
The parables then became Jesus' self-revelation to his Church.
They continue to retain his presence, his power, his mystery.
By preserving these images Matthew helps the Church keep
alive its end-time faith that Jesus will return as Bridegroom.

76

In the final parable of the kingdom of God Matthew nourishes a spirit of hope and watchfulness for that return. He offers the story of the ten virgins of the wedding party. Believers are to prepare themselves for the coming of their risen Lord just as the five prudent virgins prepared themselves for the coming of the groom (Mt 25.1-13).

TEACHING BY PARABLES IN LUKE

Please read: Luke 10.25-37

By tradition Luke has been represented as a painter. Whether he painted portraits we do not know. But he certainly does paint word pictures. Along with his vivid character portrayals in parables Luke used them to sharpen the image of Jesus as model. As wise teacher sent by God, Jesus, as portrayed by Luke, created mini-dramas capable of inspiring converts from paganism.

To give his parables greater impact Luke carefully places them in his Gospel. He frames them by significant scenes that highlight their message.

A good example is his way of dealing with the lawyer's question about conditions necessary to gain eternal life. In the Gospels of both Matthew and Mark this question occurs during the controversies leading up to the betrayal of Jesus. Jesus answers it simply in terms of God's command to love one another.

Into this framework Luke inserts the parable of the good Samaritan. The love that fulfills God's law does good to others without placing restrictions. The lawyer was looking for certain qualifications within others to make them worthy of his love.

Jesus rejects that approach and insists that a believer's love be universal and spontaneous. It imitates God's compassion toward all. In this parable Jesus links two realities that his audience were not capable of associating—to be good and to be a Samaritan. Jewish hostility prevented them from seeing any good in the heretical group of Samaritans.

For Luke this parable is a continual question for his readers. It forced them to see themselves as beggars in the ditch in need of God's compassion in Jesus to be brought back to life. And it still speaks to today's readers. It becomes an ongoing call to imitate Jesus. "Go and do likewise" (Lk 10.37).

A DIFFICULT LUKAN PARABLE

Please read: Luke 16.1-13

Ordinarily Luke treats each parable as a distinct and unique picture. He avoids stringing them together as Matthew does in his great chapter of kingdom parables (Mt 13.1-51). Luke prefers to link parables with wisdom sayings so that the one may clarify the other.

A good example is the difficult parable of the evil manager (Lk 16.1-7). The anti-hero has been enriching himself instead of his employer. Now he has been exposed! What can he do to provide for his future?

This crisis galvanizes him into creative action for the first time in many years. In the short period at his disposal he insures for himself a viable future. He makes deals with all his owner's debtors that reduce their debts. This is his response to a crisis situation.

The parable itself ends with the description of his clever manipulation of the books. Like all parables it is open-ended. Its revelation is not complete until it moves the readers to act. How am I doing in terms of eternal destiny?

But what about the manager's unscrupulous way of providing for himself? The example obviously caused problems for Christian preachers. As they told the parable they applied it to other situations. Luke has gathered up a whole collection of these sayings and placed them at the end of the parable (16.8-13). He translates a parable of end-time crisis into a moral exhortation.

PARABLES AND DISCIPLESHIP

Please read: Matthew 13.51-52

The revelation of the mystery in parables is never finished. They remain the cutting edge of the kingdom as it addresses each new generation. Each audience hears in a different way. These choice fruits of Jesus' creativity convert everyday banality into the poetry of God's healing.

At the end of his sermon on the parables of the kingdom Matthew pictures Jesus turning to his disciples. He asks them if they understood what he was saying. When they say "yes," he reminds them of their responsibility as stewards of the kingdom. They are to make available to others things new and old out of the wisdom of the kingdom (Mt 13.52).

Revelation is for service. Jesus had already reminded the Pharisees, "The good person makes good things available from his good treasure" (12.35). The power of parables continually invites believers to prayerful dialogue with the heart of Jesus. The presence of his Spirit enables them to meet the new challenges facing the Church in the world.

Since each person confronts unique problems, parables do not say the same thing to each one. Yet they still build bridges from the incarnate Jesus to every age. From the hope they give the Church has courage to say, "Thy kingdom come."

SUGGESTIONS FOR REFLECTION

1. How did you formerly describe a parable? What new insights did this chapter give you about parables?

2. How are the parables a form of "revelation"?

3. The evangelists give many reasons why Jesus taught in parables. Instead of limiting themselves to one reason, realizing that there was truth in each, they left us with a variety of reasons. How does the Church use this approach to theology today?

4. We look to Jesus as a master-teacher whom we would like to imitate. Yet we think of him as one-of-a-kind. How did his style of teaching differ from that of other good teachers? Select one parable and show how he used it to invite us to a change of heart.

5. "Parables are miracles in words." Why is the parable in Luke 18.9-14 considered a miracle of healing and hope in words?

6. Select one parable and note how Matthew and Luke placed it, linked it, and used it differently.

7. Why is every parable open-ended? What is the special invitation to the hearer in the parables of the good Samaritan and the unjust steward? Is the message the same for each one of us?

CHAPTER VII

GOD HEALS THROUGH JESUS

As the second form of divine revelation, miracles provide an important supplement to parables. The two contribute to an understanding of each other as well as clarifying the religious nature of revelation.

A natural bridge between the two is provided by symbolic acts of Jesus. For example, Jesus cleansed the temple to show it was to be reverenced as his Father's house. He ate with sinners as a sign that God was offering salvation to all. Miracles are parables in action that grant access to the path of salvation.

Just as a parable is understood only in conversion, so a miracle is witnessed as revelation only in an act of faith. It is not a piece of magic to dazzle or force consent from unwilling spectators. Rather it is an intimate invitation to enter God's kingdom as manifest in Jesus as Messiah.

Miracles then are signs in the context of faith for they make available to the humble of heart a share in Christ's power. They show that his ministry ushers in the final age and provides a foretaste of his glorification. The reality they signify is twofold, namely, the fullness of end-time power and the fuller justice that Jesus offers his followers.

Biblical miracles are not like the marvels of space exploration or television or modern medicine. They assume the personal activity of God in all levels of reality—in the blessings of nature, in

physical health, in human genius. God makes all nature serve
those he loves as his own.

Miracles are God's way of telling his chosen people that they can
and should expect his support. Only he has power to bring them
to the destiny he prepared, and he wants to use that power for
their salvation. They can trust him.

MIRACLES OF JESUS WERE CONTROVERSIAL

Please read: Mark 2.1—3.6

Of all the evangelists Mark devotes the most space in proportion
to the length of his Gospel to miracles. Through the first part of
Mark Jesus stands forth as one who makes God's presence available through mighty deeds. This manner of acting manifested
the kingdom of God at work to overcome forces of evil in the
world.

Traditional stories of how Jesus performed exorcisms, that is,
drove out demons, were suitable for Mark's purpose. In themselves such marvelous deeds are open to a variety of interpretations. Mark is careful that his readers understand them as acts of
revelation. He does so in two ways:

(1) He integrates these deeds of Jesus into the shaping principle
of his Gospel. Along with the parables of Jesus they manifest
the divine wisdom and power he possesses as God's chosen one.
Significantly, when Mark talks about Jesus going around teaching, he may actually describe his working a cure. Such an action reveals the "authority" of his wisdom (Mk 2.12).

(2) Mark structures individual miracles stories in a clear, distinctive style to highlight the nature of Jesus' saving power. They
open with a picture of someone in need asking the help of Jesus either directly or indirectly. For example, Peter's mother-
in-law is sick with a fever. The by-standers inform Jesus as he
enters the house (Mk 1.29-30).

Next, Jesus intervenes with a display of authority in word or
action. Thus, he takes the feverish woman by the hand and
lifts her from the bed. Finally comes the proof of divine intervention. Peter's mother-in-law is able to stand and wait on the
guests (1.31).

In the course of apostolic preaching before Mark wrote his Gospel, the accounts of the miracles of Jesus were put into a form
effective for proclaiming the good news. They were embellished
with elements to indicate theological insight or apologetic
thrust. Mark often incorporates such motifs into his accounts
of miracles.

For example, Jesus defends his attitude toward the Sabbath by
saying, "The Son of Man is Lord even of the Sabbath" (Mk2.28).
Immediately Mark gives an account of a cure on the Sabbath
to affirm this authority.

Mark's way of arranging scenes points to the miracles of Jesus
as a cause of controversy between him and Jewish authorities.
After the first burst of popularity that Jesus experienced and
the large crowds he attracted, Mark indicates a change toward
him. Mark records a series of five scenes to show growing resentment by Jewish authorities.

The first scene is the cure of the paralytic. Because of the large
crowd he has to be let down on a stretcher through the roof of
the house where Jesus is teaching. Here the conflict arises because Jesus affirms the man's sins are forgiven. His opponents
accuse him of playing God (Mk 2.1-12).

The final scene of this mini-series is the incident mentioned
above about a cure on the Sabbath. It results in the first step
in a conspiracy against Jesus. The Pharisees and the followers
of Herod agree to join forces to bring about his downfall (3.6).

The reason for Mark's arrangement of the miracle episodes is to keep before his readers the nature of the revelation Jesus brings In the midst of his mighty deeds Jesus proclaims his purpose. "I did not come to call the upright, but sinners" (Mk 2.17). Hi displays of divine power are calls to religious decision.

The ministry of Jesus forced his hearers to take sides for or against Jesus. The Gospel of Mark re-enacts the same drama. Readers must either believe and accept Jesus as God's chosen one or reject his offer of salvation.

MATTHEW'S SECTION ON MIRACLES

Please read: Matthew 8.1—9.35

Matthew wants his readers to consider the section 4.23—9.35 as a unit. His literary method of saying that is the "inclusion" between the opening and closing verses. An inclusion is the technique of rounding out a unit of material by referring back to its opening. In this case Matthew pictures Jesus as going around Galilee "teaching in their synagogues and proclaiming the good news of the kingdom and healing every disease and every sickness."

The material enclosed in this section by Matthew is the Sermon of the Mount and a detailed narration of ten healing miracles of Jesus. The unit then is a mini-Gospel. It pictures Jesus revealing the kingdom of God in word and deed.

Jesus begins by an extended proclamation of the new law of God's reign. Then he demonstrates his authority to speak for God by these acts of authority. The Sermon of the Mount is a comprehensive statement of the ethical demands of God's will The series of miracles demonstrate God's almighty power is avai able to achieve that will.

Matthew's method of grouping his material shows he is not inte ested in purely physical effects but in the symbolic role of Jesus actions. These deeds are symbols both in number and in kind. The number ten symbolizes fullness of divine power. The range of cures denotes omnipotence. He heals leprosy, fever, blindness, deafness, paralysis, hemorrhage. He even raises from the dead and drives out demons.

These ten healings make up half of all the miracles Matthew records. The concentration has an impact similar to his long sermons. It impresses upon readers the authority of Jesus and the revelation he brings.

Most of these ten cures are in the other synoptic Gospels but this arrangement heightens the impact. Matthew begins with the cure of a leper. No doubt this is put first because Jesus commands the leper to go and show himself as cured to the Jewish priest. He is to offer the gift prescribed in the law of Moses as witness to the healing.

Jesus said he came to fulfill the law. Matthew makes his first miracles a demonstration that he does not disregard the customs of his people. His power too comes from the unique God of Israel. His ministry is destined to be a new and more intimate healing presence of God.

MIRACLES AND DISCIPLES

This extended arrangement of ten cures by Matthew points to the existence of earlier collections telling of the miracles of Jesus. Preachers in the apostolic Church must have made up small units that were helpful in evangelization.

The scenes in Matthew 8.1-18 make up a day of healing in the city of Capernaum. It ends in the evening with large groups of the sick and those possessed by demons being brought to Jesus to be healed. Matthew rounds out this day with one of his typical fulfillment quotations.

Matthew comments that this healing ministry of Jesus fulfills the prophecy of Isaiah about the Suffering Servant of the Lord. He took upon himself the weaknesses of his people (Mt 8.17). This verse is a good example of Matthew's freedom in adapting biblical texts to illustrate the saving power of Jesus.

That saving power is not limited to the earthly career of Jesus but through his Church extends into all generations and places. The ongoing dimension of Jesus as Immanuel (God with us) explains Matthew's insertion of scenes about discipleship in this miracles section. The revelation of Jesus demands total commitment to him and a break with the world's goals.

When people set limits to their following him, Jesus quotes or coins a proverb, "Let the dead bury their own dead" (8.22). He is not passing moral judgment on different lifestyles but giving a graphic picture of end-time urgency. The present age is passing away. Those called to faith in the kingdom of God must not lose this chance of salvation.

Included in this unit is the story of Matthew's own call and the banquet he offered for his tax collector friends. They were considered sinners by the law-abiding Pharisees. Jesus uses the occasion to teach the real goal of revelation—the call of sinners to salvation. It is not abstract theory but a sharing of God's mercy (Mt 9.12-13).

By this creative handling of the miracles of Jesus Matthew has provided his readers with an insight for appreciating the liberating power of the kingdom of God. The freedom it gives empowers sinners to commit themselves to God.

IN LUKE MIRACLES ELICIT FAITH

Please read: Luke 5.1-11

In absolute numbers Luke describes the largest number of miracles (Lk-20; Mt-19; Mk-18). But Luke is the longest of the Gospels. So proportionately he gives the smallest amount of space to miracles.

In keeping with his goal of an "orderly account," Luke fixes a balance between the teaching and the mighty deeds of Jesus as revealing God's reign. Because of his audience he has to exercise care in the way he presents miracles. Jesus did not perform them as magic feats to dazzle the crowds. His goal was to arouse repentance and encourage trust in God.

Luke's description of the call of the first disciples is a good illustration of this concern. Jesus began to preach in Galilee and was attracting a large audience. Crowds pressed around him so tightly on the shore of the lake that he asked Simon to let him get in his boat and preach a little distance from the shore.

After preaching Jesus tells Simon to row out further and throw out the nets for a catch. Simon had been fishing all night without success. Yet he obeys and immediately makes a large haul (Lk 5.5-7). At this point Luke introduces the second name Peter. He was overcome with religious awe and responds to this miracle with an act of humility. He is unworthy to be in the presence of Jesus. Instead, Jesus invites him and his companions to becomes sharers in his saving work.

This same rhythm in Luke's presentation of miracles occurs in his call of Levi. Jesus is preaching and healing. A group of men bring in a paralytic. This is the same cure Mark records. The man is lowered through the roof. Jesus forgives his sins. The Pharisees complain. Luke adds that the crowd is filled with joy and wonder because, "We have seen marvels today!" (Lk 5.26).

Jesus immediately goes out and sees the tax collector Levi and invites him, "Follow me." He obeys at once, because he has seen the power of Jesus. It is this power that offers him hope for salvation.

RESPONSE TO JESUS AS EXAMPLE

Please read: Luke 17.11-19

It is characteristic of Luke's method in describing miracles to include a comment from the person cured. Take the incident of the ten lepers that Luke alone preserves. They had to keep away from people. So they shouted, "Jesus, Master, have mercy on us" (17.13).

Jesus did not make any dramatic gesture. He simply tells them to report to the priest. This was to receive a clean bill of health to return to society. On the way they notice they are cleansed. One of them is so happy that he starts to praise God and runs back to Jesus to thank him.

Jesus comments on the failure of the others to glorify God. Only for this Samaritan has the healing opened up the true healing of faith. By including a description of similar responses Luke invites his readers to value the healing power of God in Jesus.

This power is above all compassionate. Only Luke pictures Jesus in an expression of that spontaneous compassion toward the widow who lost her only son. Without being asked, Jesus approached and gave him back to her (Lk 7.11-17).

Like the other evangelists Luke shows that the miracles of Jesus evoked diverse responses. Many who were cured praised God. But the Pharisees took a belligerent attitude. They began to challenge Jesus to give them signs in nature.

Jesus refused to play with that kind of approach. He knew that the kingdom of God does not come "with observation," as if it could be controlled. If they truly open their eyes, they will see that it is already at work in their midst (Lk 17.20-21). God is already healing through Jesus. His power expresses the religious response to God that his disciples practice.

Those hostile to Jesus accuse him of working wonders through the power of the demon Beelzebul when he casts an unclean spirit out of a man who could not speak (Lk 11.14-15). Jesus reminds them that their teachers also perform exorcisms. So they had to search their own motivation for opposing him.

Luke writes with an awareness that many wonder workers were traveling around the Roman Empire. Large crowds went to popular healing shrines. His readers were acquainted with the practice. It was important that the miracles of Jesus be distinguished from them. He comes to test the deepest motives of human hearts.

In Luke's Gospel as Jesus draws near to his passion the number of miracle accounts decreases. But not his healing power. Only Luke notes that Jesus cured the ear of the servant in the Garden of Olives after Peter had cut it off (22.51). His power to heal is now available to all through his saving death and resurrection.

HOW MIRACLES SPEAK TODAY

A reading of the synoptic Gospels makes clear that miracles are meaningful only in a context of faith. They were written with a religious purpose in mind for people who saw reality as a whole. They saw creation as totally subject to God's power. They expected divine intervention and celebrated it. His provident concern hovered over all his works.

All of that, of course, is a far cry from the scientific world in which we live, a world of technology and specialization. The difference accounts for our modern difficulty in dealing with biblical miracles.

The cult of progress through empirical research often obscures a sense of the sacred. The loss of a sense of wholeness has fragmented society. True appreciation of the miracles of Jesus as portrayed in the Gospel offers a way to bring healing to our tortured world.

SUGGESTIONS FOR REFLECTION

1. If "parables are miracles in words," could you also say "miracles are parables"?

2. What do the miracles of Jesus reveal about God's saving power in all of creation? What do they reveal of God's relationship to those he has chosen as his own? Who are the "chosen ones"?

3. How did Jesus' miracles lend support to his teachings? In Mark's Gospel how did his audiences react to the miracles? Why are we told "His displays of divine power are calls to religious decision" and "His ministry is destined to be a new and more intimate healing presence of God?"

4. In the cure of ten lepers (Luke 17.11-19) why is faith called "the true healing"? Which two miracles are described by Luke alone?

5. Are you aware of miracles today? If today's miracles are signs of God's saving power, what miracles in your own life are presently forcing you to take sides for or against Jesus?

6. Do you really believe in miracles?

7. Have you ever experienced the healing presence of God?

CHAPTER VIII

THE PASSION REVEALS TRUE LOVE

A reading of the first part of Mark's Gospel points to Jesus as the one who reveals his Father by words of wisdom and by mighty deeds. He seems to be the "divine man" miracle worker. His feats are capable of attracting a large following.

Mark is careful not to leave readers with that image of Jesus. Very early on he notes that the enemies of Jesus started to form a scheme to destroy him (Mk 3.6). Jesus devoted himself to proclaiming the kingdom of God and to calling his hearers to conversion and faith in the good news (Mk 1.15).

Often Jesus was misunderstood. He rejected Peter's designation of him as Messiah because it assumed a political orientation of his work. All the Gospels show that the mission of Jesus cannot be explained within human horizons. It was an act of God's saving will to reconcile the human race to himself.

As Mark's Gospel progresses it becomes clear this goal is to be achieved in a paradoxical way. Jesus is destined to be resisted for fidelity to his God-given mission. How could the heavenly Father lead his Son into such a situation? This is the question that the Gospels force us to confront.

INEVITABILITY OF THE PASSION

Please read: Mark 8.31-33

The second half of Mark's Gospel opens on a theme that centers the activity of Jesus on his suffering and death. Jesus predicts that these must take place.

Jesus makes this revelation only to his disciples rather than to the crowds. Mark presents him as doing this on three different occasions (Mk 8.31-33; 9.30-32; 10.32-34). Even so, his disciples never fully grasp the tragedy involved. Only after his resurrection were they able to come to terms with the divine decree. After long effort they recognized that the Son of Man "had" to be put to death.

In what sense was the death of Jesus unavoidable? How could he continue in a mission that he saw was moving inexorably toward that tragic goal and still trust and hope?

He must have seen hidden depths in the Father's plan that made him submit lovingly to such a fate. Jesus saw his whole life as responding to the will of a loving Father. All his words to the crowds proclaimed God's loving care for his children. God makes his sun and rain available to good and evil without distinction (Mt 5.48). Jesus experienced God as good.

Jesus also knew from the start that evil exists in the world and that it often triumphs. The universal penetration of evil reveals the human race as enslaved to sin. A slavish mentality prevails. If mortals are to be liberated from that trap, they must be convinced of God's love for them. They must see his concern translated into an overpowering love enticing them back to his friendship.

As his enemies yielded to the destructive power of sin, Jesus became the center of the struggle between good and evil. He identified completely with his Father's saving love. Soon he saw his mission in terms of pronouncing a loving "no" against sin's power to destroy.

God was calling Jesus to turn back the tide of sin by being the one in whom he would reconcile creatures to himself. The death of Jesus would be the visible expression of the Father's saving will as it triumphs over the alienating force of sin.

From the Gospel narratives it is not possible to reconstruct how Jesus actually came to this understanding. For the Gospel writers the exact historical unfolding was not important.

JESUS' GROWING AWARENESS THAT HE MUST SUFFER

Mark makes clear that Jesus saw his mission as response to God's acting in him. His response was not for himself alone but was to represent humanity's hope. It is an invitation to all to become his disciples and children of his Father.

To accept this invitation means to embrace a form of life conformed to the mind of Jesus in accepting his cross. "If anyone wishes to come after me, he must deny himself, take up his cross and follow me" (Mk 8.34).

Jesus' triple prediction of his passion serves as the key factor in Mark's structuring the second half of his Gospel. This is Mark's way of saying that Jesus became increasingly aware of the implications of his mission. He would have to proclaim it publicly in Jerusalem. His Father sent him to make the kingdom available to all and he was to carry out this mission by obedience.

Jesus recognized himself as unique among humans. He was God's Son who alone enjoyed full communion with the Father's will. Since other humans were estranged from God, his words would inevitably lead to confrontation. Reconciliation to God could not be accomplished on a surface level by speeches. A much more profound message had to be communicated.

Jesus could deliver the message of God's saving love only in the language of the cross. Mark's repetition of the passion predictions dramatizes where the antagonism between God's goodness and human sinfulness must lead.

Sin drives humans to reject their God. To proclaim this truth was to provoke growing anger and resentment. As a result, Jesus saw he must let this torrent of sin engulf him and carry him off. To do so required love and trust. It was the heart of the Father's plan to reconcile his creatures.

Obedience to that plan demanded that Jesus surrender all his desire for personal safety and let sin have power over him. The unselfishness of his act will reveal the power of divine love to confront, confound and overcome human sinfulness. Cross redemption becomes the act that makes divine freedom available to human hearts.

This growing consciousness that he must suffer does not mean Jesus was in any sense at odds with his Father's will. God's aim was not to punish Jesus but to save sinners.

Jesus came to a humanity that was in a slavish condition, unable to recognize God's love for it. The inability of humanity to accept him as God's representative was a sign that it is flawed and in need of redemption. His overpowering act of love remains capable of opening channels of communication, trust and hope in every human heart.

True, the synoptic Gospels do not speculate on the self-consciousness of Jesus as he approached his death. Their literary form as narratives made that type of theologizing impossible. The evangelists are careful, however, to affirm the identification of Jesus with the Father's will in all that he undertook and endured.

He is a prophet who must die in the holy city of Jerusalem (Lk 13.33). Such obedience becomes the sign God uses to restore to humans true freedom—the ability to love without self-ishness.

JESUS LOYALLY ACCEPTS HIS MISSION

Please read: Matthew 23.1-39

The Gospels indicate that for the most part the cross sought Jesus, not that he sought the cross. He did not act in an arrogant way toward his own people who were to betray him. It is true he attacked his enemies. But his attacks were on their abuse of authority, their desire to be esteemed as better than others. Their actions were oppressive of the poor and weak. "For they speak and do not do" (Mt 23.3).

Worst of all, they barred the kingdom to others (Mt 23.13). They saw Jesus as a threat to their authority over the people. His method of interpreting the law of Moses showed him as superior to it. So they were afraid.

As Jesus saw that full-scale confrontation was impending, he became more assertive. Matthew gathers together in a series of seven woes the complaints Jesus addressed to the Jewish leaders as hypocrites. They were blind to the deeper realities of spirit. They could not open themselves to the mystery of God's saving plan.

By remaining on the surface level of God's will as expressed in the commands of the law, they missed its important goals, "judgment and mercy and loyalty" (Mt 23.23).

In the face of such blindness Matthew has Jesus speak his last public words to the people in the form of a lament over the chosen city of Jerusalem. Jesus compares his love for it to that of a mother bird. How anxious is he to gather his brood under his wings! But they refuse. They will pay a high price.

Despite all these criticisms Jesus still upholds the authority of the scribes and Pharisees. They hold positions on the chair of

Moses. So their words are to be obeyed. Jesus knows at the same time his attacks will galvanize them into action.

Ultimately then it is clear that Jesus knew what he was doing. His open loyalty to his mission sets the opposition against him. He knows a clash will necessarily result if he keeps on the course he has chosen. And he continues!

JESUS' ATTITUDE TOWARD HIS DEATH

This stance of Jesus toward his opponents was an integral part of the divine necessity. The Father did not decree that his Son should die unwillingly or as totally passive. Jesus saw and accepted violent death because he loved and trusted his Father, because he loved and felt compassion for fellow human beings (see Gal 2.20).

In the face of sin this was a deliberate and necessary choice. Even when the moment was upon him and his spirit shuddered at the thought, Jesus refused to ask the Father for help to avoid it. He made his decision on behalf of humanity to liberate mortals from the fatal grasp of evil.

Jesus made the decision to submit himself to those wishing to put him to death because he was convinced the Father willed him to do so. He trusted both his knowledge of the Father and God's power to make his death a saving event.

Not that the Father wanted Jesus killed. His death became a necessity only in the context of humanity's alienation from God. Only God could break down the barrier sin had erected. The one power capable of achieving reconciliation was an outpouring of unselfish love. Jesus, in perfect communion with his Father, willingly made that act of love.

MARK'S ACCOUNT OF THE TRIAL OF JESUS

Please read: Mark 14.53–15.20

Mark's account of the trial narrative brings together many themes
of his Gospel. His genius is evident in his ability to reconcile
the paradoxes of Jesus' life.

As a guiding literary model Mark draws upon Old Testament
traditions of the suffering just man. In particular, he shows Jesus as the Suffering Servant of the Lord. This was an ideal figure in the book of Isaiah to show God's power to vindicate
those who trust in him.

Mark skillfully incorporates such themes into his passion narrative. As a result, to be understood it must be reflected upon
in prayer and faith. Jesus suffers as the last in a long line of
obedient servants sent by God to his people. Mark was the first
Christian author to assemble early traditions into a unified theological narrative destined to guide the Church in its liturgical
celebration of the Lord's death.

Many of these themes are evident in Mark's account of the trial
of Jesus. He makes what was probably the judicial procedure
of booking Jesus by Jewish authorities into a full-blown trial
and condemnation.

Three elements in his reconstruction of the scene are meant to
instruct believers about the religious meaning of these events in
the redemptive mission of Jesus:

(1) the insertion of the trial between two scenes featuring St.
Peter (14.54 and 14.66-72). The contrast is deliberate. While
Peter is making himself comfortable, Jesus is subjected to weari-
some questioning. While Jesus loyally proclaims himself as God's

Son, Peter denies he ever knew him. Even the disciple is in need of salvation. Without the loyalty of the suffering Jesus, none of the apostles' gifts are of any avail.

(2) the word of Jesus about the temple. Mark indicates that the witnesses could not put into understandable words what Jesus said about his relation to the temple (14.58). Actually, he has put profound theological language into their mouths. He reminds his readers that Jesus is the center of all true worship of the Father.

Why does Mark incorporate these exchanges that end without resolution? His interest is not in historical details of accusations against Jesus. Mark here gives implications of Jesus' stand against temple worship.

This scene recalls Jesus' cleansing of the temple after he had solemnly entered Jerusalem. By that act Jesus symbolized that the temple cult was no longer pleasing to his Father. The Jews were incapable of understanding how such a situation could be possible. Only believing Christians can identify the risen Jesus as living temple through whom God is glorified.

Mark again alludes to this transfer of worship after he tells of the death of Jesus. The veil of the temple is split from top to bottom. By exposing the secret place, God has profaned the Jewish mysteries and rendered them ineffective. The new temple is the believing community in Jesus.

(3) the unveiling of the messianic secret. Now that the danger of misunderstanding is past, Jesus tells the high priest that he is indeed Son of God.

Jesus shows he uses this term in a unique sense by identifying himself also as Son of Man (14.61-62). Throughout his Gospel Mark has associated this title with the sufferings of Jesus. The passion will provide the occasion for God to manifest his approval of Jesus' obedience and to bring about the kingdom.

Jesus proclaims himself as the heaven-sent apocalyptic leader of God's chosen people. He is ready to face death as the liberator destined to inaugurate the new age.

This trial narrative of Mark is a striking illustration of the nature of Gospel. It is a call to believers to identify with the loyal Jesus and to follow him on the road to Calvary. This is the journey of faith. True faith always blossoms into unbounded hope and joyful witness to God's saving power.

MARK'S THEOLOGY OF THE CROSS

Please read: Mark 8.34—9.1

The way Mark constructs his narrative of the passion shows how the cross is central to the Gospel. The richness of detail and concentration of theological themes as well as its length makes it the most important part of his story. In fact, the cross has dominated the Gospel since the first passion prediction. Even before that, Mark pointed to the tragic fate of Jesus.

Obviously Mark did not create that theology. Paul long before proclaimed Jesus crucified as "God's power and God's wisdom" (1 Cor 1.24). But the Gospel of Mark provides the first integrated narrative proclaiming the theology of the cross for the Church's liturgical celebrations.

In practical terms, this Gospel is an invitation to believers to celebrate the cross pattern of existence. Jesus' choice of it shapes the life of his Church and the lifestyle of all his disciples.

Mark tells us this by the arrangement spoken of in Chapter III. Each of the passion predictions is followed by a discourse on discipleship. Let me elaborate briefly on this identification of discipleship with the word of the cross. His method is the use of a three-element development.

The three elements are:
(1) a prediction of the passion by Jesus,

(2) lack of comprehension by his disciples,

(3) a mini-sermon on the cross as pattern for discipleship.

THREE SERMONS ON THE CROSS

In the first of these sermons the reader finds a view of the cross as purifying and enlightening. Jesus asks that his followers motivate their lives by the love that prompted him to give all for the good news. This sermon is basically a revelation that the wisdom of the cross is superior to worldly values. To embrace the cross is to reject a "sinful and adulterous generation" (Mk 8.38). This loyal stance will enjoy the vision of the Son of Man returning in glory.

The second mini-sermon on discipleship celebrates the paradox of the cross (9.33-37). The disciples were still thinking of the kingdom in terms of political power and their share in it.

Jesus counters by placing a little child in their midst as representing the kingdom. To receive him and share in his victory they must find him in the vulnerable little child. All the more, then, those wishing to proclaim the kingdom must strip themselves of all and become as children.

The final mini-sermon contrasts the ambition of the disciples with the humble service demanded by a life patterned upon the cross (10.42-45). This is the style Jesus adopted in coming not to be served but to serve, that is, to be obedient always to his Father's will to save all.

LUKE'S EMPHASES IN HIS PASSION ACCOUNT

Please read: Luke 23.26-49

Luke shows that Mark's account of the passion had to be adapted to meet the needs of converts from paganism. We can show how he modifies the account of the crucifixion.

He keeps his emphasis on Jesus as model for human conduct. His narrative shows the Lord as exemplar for qualities of life his readers need—confidence in God, compassion, forgiveness, a spirit of prayer.

As Jesus advanced toward Calvary, Luke notes that Simon was pressed into service to carry the cross "after Jesus." He thus becomes the image of every disciple. Jesus goes forth to death confidently, telling the women not to cry.

Only Luke pictures Jesus as praying for those who nailed him to the cross. As persecutions increased in the Roman Empire, Christians would have many occasions to imitate their Lord's forgiveness. Also, Luke alone writes about the repentant thief and his prayer to be remembered. Jesus responds with an expression of confidence in God's powerful care for him and his own ability to save sinners.

Jesus himself seems to determine the moment for ending his self-sacrificing death. He confidently speaks to his Father in a verse from Psalm 31, "Into your hands I place my spirit."

The bystanders speak for the whole world. The centurion says that Jesus was a "just man," and innocent servant of God. The people in the crowd acknowledge their guilt by striking their breasts. They recognize the conduct of Jesus as a revelation of his perfect union with the heavenly Father.

INTERPRETING THE PASSION TODAY

Please read: Mark 15.21-41

A careful reading of the passion narratives of the synoptic Gospels makes clear their nature as religious interpretations of the power of Christ's death. They treat it as more than a past historical event. Jesus dies to reveal himself as Son of God (Mk 15.39). His death shattered the veil of the temple and makes available a new convenant in his own blood.

This is an event of universal and ongoing consequences. These simple narratives convey profound theological depth. They have generated many theories of atonement. The Church does not define theological positions but articles of faith. The presence of God to Jesus in his obedient suffering becomes the means of bringing believers into eternal life.

The crucifixion as central event in human destiny reaches out universally through the reality of the resurrection. The risen Jesus becomes Lord and Head of the Church.

His new existence is such that he incorporates all who believe in him as members of his Body. As literary creations the Gospels offer readers authentic interpretations of the mystery of Jesus. He is exemplary symbol and integrating core of all true discipleship. To accept his cross is to be his disciple.

The death of Jesus was a unique act. It is also universal in an infinite variety of ways for it is the good news that frees both humanity as a whole and individuals from the enslaving consequences of sin. This death acts not simply as model but as power in weakness to offer hope and peace.

Christians continue to speak the language of the cross by interiorizing the death of Jesus as their life principle today. This means
—drawing inspiration and support from it for personal and communal existence,
—making it the model of community consciousness and direction in carrying out the responsibility of today's living,
—celebrating it in worship as the healing and unifying force of Christ's presence to the world.

SUGGESTIONS FOR REFLECTION

1. What is a paradox? Why are the mission, passion, and death of Jesus called paradoxical?

2. "God's aim was not to punish Jesus but to save sinners."
Is this the way you have always thought of God when you considered the crucifixion? How could Jesus see his Father's will
as loving and saving toward him?

3. In your lifetime have you ever freely accepted pain, suffering, loss, or inconvenience because you loved another person
more than your own comfort? If so, notice the parallel between
this and the way Jesus preferred his Father's will to save.

4. You have read, "Jesus became obedient unto death, even
the death of the cross." How have you explained this? What
new insights have you gained from this chapter?

5. "True freedom (is) the ability to love without selfishness."
Is this the way most Americans speak of "freedom"? Why was
Jesus truly free in his crucifixion and death? Are you growing
in true freedom?

6. What was the real blindness of the Pharisees in advocating
the law? What advice does Jesus give the people about obey-
ing them? Has this any application for us today?

7. In Galatians 2.19 Paul says he died to the law to live for God.
How is this possible? What relationship has it to the death of
Jesus? Give an example in the Church today to show a lessened
emphasis on law and a greater stress on living for God.

8. If Mark's Gospel "is an invitation to believers to celebrate
the cross pattern of existence," where is the cross in your life
as a Christian? Can you celebrate it? Is it a "purifying and
enlightening experience"? Is it a humbling experience? Is it
leading you to greater wisdom about life values? Is it for you
a mercy of God?

9. In Luke 23.26-49, what are three ways the author shows
Jesus as a model for human conduct?

10. Why do we explain Jesus' death as "good news"? What is the "power" it released? In what ways can there be power in dying? Give examples based on scenes of death you have seen or heard about.

11. Give examples of how Christians interiorize the death of Jesus as their life principle today.

CHAPTER IX

CONFIRMATION OF
THE GOOD NEWS

Please read: Mark 16.1-8

All the Gospels reach their climax with the resurrection of Jesus. Yet no one saw him rise from the dead. The Gospels insist upon the truth that his resurrection is a mystery. It was not an event that could be hemmed in by time and space.

As a mystery it is made known not by human insight but by divine revelation. So it can be accepted only through faith. That is why the evangelists never try to describe the event itself. Rather they relate what changes took place in Jesus and in the believing community because of this mystery.

A transforming change was evident in both Jesus and his followers. All the implications were not immediately evident. They became clear only in the experience of the growing Church. The Gospel accounts mark the final stage of a long period of reflection on this mystery. It went through a series of steps before being finally synthesized by the evangelists.

First of all, the language adequate to express the mystery had to be developed by Church preachers. The Gospels are the word of God in words of men. The double tension of the event is that of continuity with the earthly Jesus and transformation into his new status as Lord.

On the one hand, the risen Lord is the same Jesus who walked upon the earth. He continues to exist as true man able to relate to the needs of those who seek his help. On the other hand, Jesus is exalted at the right hand of the Father. The whole universe is subject to him.

When believers proclaim, "Jesus Christ is Lord," they mean he lives as equal to the God of Israel. The word "lives" takes on a special meaning. The risen Jesus is life-giving; he touches all reality with transforming power.

EXPERIENCE AS KEY TO KNOW THE RESURRECTION

Please read: Luke 24.32-35

The early Christians came to know this mystery not by any kind of scientific verification. The risen Jesus poured out his own Holy Spirit to transform their personal lives. This Spirit presence in the primitive believers made the Church a witness.

It was a source of light to many groping in darkness against despair and alienation. It was a sign to pagans of God's gifts to his chosen ones. Enthusiasm animated the hearts of those who believed they received new life from the One who died for them. They were children of God in Christ.

Only because of this ongoing initiative and experienced presence of Jesus through his Holy Spirit was this small community able to give witness to an ineffable event in a variety of language forms. The same mystery is celebrated from Paul's letters to the Gospel narratives.

In reading the Gospel accounts of the resurrection it is important to keep in mind that they were written after Paul's letters. They depend upon the religious insights and special vocabulary developed by the primitive community. They are not a "biography" of the risen Lord.

106

The exalted Lord is more than an inspiration to the Church. He is its very life support. Even more. Through his Spirit he makes the believing community the saving principle of the world. He was foreshadowed in the Old Covenant. He nourishes believers through his sacramental presence. He enlightens the world through the preaching of his Church.

THE RESURRECTION AS AN APOLOGETIC

Please read: Luke 24.13-31

The inbreaking of the risen Jesus upon his apostles created an overwhelming impact. Luke says that his appearance caused terror. They were sure he was dead and thought they saw a ghost (Lk 24.37). He has to reassure them and prepare them to become his witnesses.

In the case of the two disciples at Emmaus Jesus explains that what happened to him is the fulfillment of the message of all Scripture. In this scene Luke telescopes the early Church's apologetic approach in preaching to both Jews and pagans. The cross is a scandal for those who cannot see it in context of the total divine plan of salvation.

Under the guidance of the risen Jesus and his Holy Spirit the infant communities worked out apologias for their new way of life. Christians read the entire Hebrew Bible over and over in the light of the life, death and resurrection of Jesus. They found him throughout—in the law, the prophets and the wisdom writings, called the psalms by Luke (24.44).

The eyewitnesses went forth and preached the good news of salvation in Jesus—first to Jews and then to pagans.

TRANSFORMATION OF THE COSMOS

Please read: Matthew 28.1-15

Matthew's Gospel is addressed primarily to converts from Judaism. It incorporates an apologetic approach in the form of a polemic. Evidently his community faced opposition from Jewish synagogues competing for the allegiance of law-abiding Jews. This conflict accounts for some of his additions.

After the death of Jesus, Matthew spoke about the opening of tombs. After Jesus' resurrection Matthew talks about an earthquake and an angel. He records attempts by the Jewish priests to cover up the victory of Jesus over death.

In spite of such additions Matthew still insists upon the event itself as a mystery. The resurrection goes beyond his power to describe. Its impact penetrates all levels of being. The earthquake signifies its cosmic dimensions. In Jesus a new heaven and a new earth come into existence.

The angel in gleaming white garments illustrates the awesome depths of the mystery. It transports believers into the divine realm and invites them to share in the fruits of the mission of Jesus. At the same time Matthew's concern is to fortify Jewish Christians against attacks. Their fellow Jews accused Jesus of being unfaithful to their ancestral heritage.

The story was circulating that Jesus' body had been stolen by his disciples. To counter this propaganda Matthew puts in his explanation of hostility to Jesus among his own people. These details indicate some of the many implications to be drawn from the mystery of Christ's resurrection.

The victory of God over death in and through Jesus is crucial for our destiny. Yet salvation is not magic. The resurrection tells believers to be converted and change their lifestyle. To do so they must harvest fruit from this mystery by meditation on the scenes presented by the evangelists.

Please read: Matthew 28.16-20

In a real sense the resurrection is the grounding reality of the Gospels. Without it none of them would have been written.

At times we might think that the evangelists are giving us a short biography of the risen Jesus between his rising from the dead and a dramatic ascension to his Father. But a careful reading of the scenes they preserve shows their aim is much different.

These narratives are the end product of a long period of reflection beginning with the first awareness the apostles had of the mystery. First came an ability to formulate it in human language, in terms meaningful to believers. Only much later was this understanding incorporated into the narrative forms found in the Gospels.

This long growth process embraced three steps:

(1) Language had to be developed to express an ineffable mystery in human terms. That seemingly impossible task was the triumph of faith responding to revelation. Faith is the special gift that lets God become our God.

The Gospel texts indicate that even the apostles who lived so close to Jesus on earth could not always understand what he meant. After he made his risen presence available to them, they were overwhelmed and lacked words to express their new experience. They had to fill old words with new meaning, like—

"Jesus lives"—not with the kind of life we know, subject to historical uncertainty and death. He is already part of the new age that cannot die.

"Jesus is raised up"—not to die again. He has entered into another dimension of reality where death has no sting. His existence transcends history.

"Jeus is exalted"—by the power of his heavenly Father. He has been made Lord of all creation.

For eyewitnesses of Jesus in his earthly and exalted states, these simple words were enough. They kept the experience alive and nourished hope in the glorious return of Jesus. But they were not sufficient for believers of later generations. Hence the second step.

(2) The mission of eyewitnesses of the resurrection was to associate others with their faith. Their preaching was a call to conversion to the Father's saving plan in Jesus. To believe was to call upon the Holy Spirit to send his gifts on those touched by the good news. "No one can say, 'Jesus is Lord' except in the Holy Spirit" (1 Cor 12.3).

During this post-resurrection period before the Gospels were written, prayerful sharing took place. Profound spiritual growth took place as the apostles shared the resurrection experience with various groups of people.

In this interaction under the guidance of the Holy Spirit there eventually evolved a narrative to celebrate the risen Jesus. He was in glory and yet still with his followers. Two types of narratives expressed this belief. They were stories about the empty tomb and accounts of the appearances of the risen Jesus to his followers.

(3) The evangelists incorporated both types of narratives about the risen Lord into the final stage of their written Gospels. These scenes were not meant to provide a detailed history of the risen Jesus from Easter until he finally left off his visible appearances.

Their aim was rather to convey the essentials of his victory over death and its enduring significance for believers and for their mission in the world. This explains why historical details of the appearances cannot be reconciled on a purely chronological level.

These appearances were not the result of ordinary human perception. They were a special self-revelation of the risen Jesus that involved a communication of his Spirit. Readers today should not try to harmonize surface details but listen to these narratives in the context of each Gospel.

EMPTY TOMB NARRATIVES

Please read: Luke 24.1-12

St. Paul never speaks of the empty tomb of Jesus. It may seem strange then that stories about it are preserved in all four Gospels. Of themselves these stories could not prove that Jesus is risen from the dead. But once Jesus made his mastery over death known, these narratives about his tomb being empty take on special significance. Why?

Because they show us something about the nature of Christ's risen state and ultimately about our own future resurrection.

Just how this resurrection will occur is a difficult point. Scripture scholars offer a variety of explanations. This lack of unity at times causes alarm in the minds of believers but it should not be so. The Church does not define theological explanations but only mysteries of faith. Yet theologians have the responsibility of offering explanations of faith.

All their explanations fall short to some extent. But they help believers grasp the sense of mystery. This is true for narratives of the empty tomb. Once belief in the resurrection is established, the empty tomb becomes a sign. It indicates the risen life belongs not only to the soul but also to the body.

The human body of Jesus participates in his glorification. It is no longer of this earth but has been liberated from any possibility of corruption by a complete transformation. It can now share the glorious spiritual existence of Jesus.

In voluntarily accepting the destruction of his material body Jesus surrendered it to the creative power of his Father. God made his body the first born from the dead. His body becomes in some mysterious way universalized and able to support the whole Church, the body of believers.

That same love is now available to reconcile and give to all humans the life of his transformed existence.

THE APPEARANCE NARRATIVES

Please read: Luke 24.36-53

The nature of the resurrection was to affirm the abiding, saving and transforming presence of Jesus. He had passed from being within human history to a new mode of being. He was not isolated but brought into more intimate contact with believers.

Jesus had to take the initiative in revealing his new presence. This is what the appearance narratives tell us. Two types are found: official visits of Jesus to the whole group of his apostles and private appearances. The first are more important for understanding the mystery of resurrection in its relation to the Church. All of the public or official visits culminate in a commission to the apostles to carry on the work of Jesus.

Each evangelist expresses this commission in terms of his own style. Commentators agree that the appearance narratives now found in the canonical Gospel of Mark are a summary of those of the other three Gospels. They were added to complete the primitive text. It ended with the silence of the women after being told of the resurrection, "for they were afraid" (16.8).

112

That primitive ending of the oldest Greek manuscripts became too stark for Christians who expected resurrection appearances in all their official Gospels.

Luke links both forms of appearances—public and private—to a meal with Jesus and his explanation of Scripture. Luke's intent was to locate the resurrection in the context of the history of salvation. He also reminded the Church that the risen Jesus is present in a special way in the eucharistic breaking of the bread. From this common sacramental sharing believers gain wisdom and courage to bear witness to Jesus.

The two disciples at Emmaus go back to Jerusalem and tell about their meeting with the risen Lord. As they speak, Jesus appears to the apostolic band. He offers them the gift of peace—and not in the banal sense of a superficial greeting. His peace is communication of power to preach "repentance and remission of sins to all nations" (24.47). That will be their witness to the power of the resurrection.

For Matthew the great commission takes place in Galilee. This is where Jesus began his public ministry with the great Sermon on the Mount. The apostles' role is to be teachers of the whole world. Their preaching will prepare new believers for incorporation into the community by baptism.

Built into these appearances of the risen Jesus, then, is the responsibility of witness to him. Sharing the mystery of the resurrection means receiving the Holy Spirit and his power to bear public witness to Jesus.

BELIEVING THE POWER OF THE RESURRECTION
Please read: Mark 16.9-20

Belief in the resurrection of Jesus did not come easily for his apostles. This fact shocks us at first but all three synoptic evangelists make a point of insisting upon it. In doing so they lead believers to a better appreciation of this mystery. Only God can lead us into the realm of faith and to that world over which Jesus rules as Lord.

His resurrection has power to combine past, present and future into dynamic unity. The same Jesus who called and formed the first apostles is powerfully present to his Church, forming and sustaining witnesses until the end of time.

This risen Jesus permeates all dimensions of a believer's existence—body and spirit, intelligence and emotions, will and imagination. Faith recognizes the risen Jesus as Lord of the new creation, destined to receive honor and glory from all. His authority constantly evokes a faith response from all his disciples throughout the world.

The response is celebrated in liturgy, in proclaiming the word of salvation, and in the mission of love.

The power of his resurrection is the new life that the Church brings to the world. The saving mission of his incarnation is completed by Jesus through his Church as his Body. His members continue to bear the marks of his suffering and his rejection by the world. Yet they do so with world-changing hope.

Such hope does not spring from any human accomplishment. The apostles did not pick themselves up by their own bootstraps. After Jesus rose he began to share his life-giving Spirit with these weak eyewitnesses of his earthly ministry. A totally new interior dynamism was their experience of the power of the risen Jesus—now with the Father and still with them.

UNITY OF CROSS AND RESURRECTION

Faith in the risen Jesus roots life in realities beyond this world. It demanded of the apostles, and still demands, certain basic choices in lifestyle, especially to take the path of the cross. For Christians, cross and resurrection can nevermore be divided.

The resurrection of Jesus proclaims that his choice of the cross was not only pleasing to his Father for himself but also justifies all who put their trust in him as Savior. The power of his resurrection resolves tension between the sense of alienation from the world's selfish spirit and yet a willing outreach toward it. Like the Master, believers maintain a spirit of compassion toward a hostile world.

To make such a gesture involves the risk of being rejected and misunderstood. Something of this tension is found in the remark of Matthew about the eleven apostles when they saw the risen Jesus in Galilee. "But they doubted" (Mt 28.17).

This mysterious comment is perhaps better rendered in English as, "Yet they hesitated." The act of faith in the risen Lord always remains a free act. God attracts but does not force the human will. For believers the power of the resurrection remains an appeal.

Through his Spirit and his sacraments the risen Jesus appeals to believers not to hesitate to embrace the cross. Only by breaking with all earthly security will they enter with him into the kingdom of God.

SUGGESTIONS FOR REFLECTION

1. Describe what you have meant when you said, "He rose from the dead." How does it agree with the sentence, "No one saw him rise from the dead . . . his resurrection is a mystery"?

2. Catholics used to study "Proofs of the Resurrection." What light does this chapter throw upon such types of explanation?

3. Is there any relation between "a transforming change was evident in both Jesus and his followers," and today's Church?

4. The Spirit presence in the early believers became for them a source of light and enthusiasm; and a sign to their pagan neighbors of God's gifts. Is this how the world perceives the Church today? Why or why not?

5. Do you think your friends and family see themselves as "the believing community which is the saving principle of the world" in our times? How would you describe yourself as a member of the believing community? What are you doing about it?

6. As with the early Christians who had their eyes opened to meaning "under the guidance of the risen Jesus and his Holy Spirit," have you ever had a person or experience take on a whole new meaning?

7. Re-read and meditate on the passages of Luke 24.13-31 and Matthew 28.11-15 to note the elements of mystery (not magic) in them and the meaning they have for your life.

8. Compare an overwhelming experience you have had—great beauty, sense of awe, immense sadness—with the reality of the witnesses of the risen Christ and their difficulty with words (Mt 28.1-10).

9. How does the "empty tomb" throw light on: resurrection of the body and soul, glorification, incorruptibility, total surrender to the Father, and the power of love?

10. "Each evangelist expresses the commission (to the apostles to carry on the work of Jesus) in terms of his own style." What are the distinct stylistic characteristics of Matthew, Mark and Luke?

11. How do today's Church members complete the saving mission of Jesus?

12. At Mass we regularly wish each other "Peace." Jesus left this gift with the apostles to be "communication of power to preach 'repentance and remission of sins to all nations.'" Can you tie this meaning in with the gift you give and receive in the liturgy?

SUGGESTIONS FOR FURTHER READING

Paul J. Achtemeier. *Mark.* Philadelphia: Fortress Press, 1975.

Madeleine Boucher. *The Mysterious Parable: A Literary Study.* Washington, D.C.: Catholic Biblical Association, 1977.

Edward J. Ciuba. *Who Do You Say That I Am? An Adult Inquiry into the First Three Gospels.* New York: Alba House, 1974.

Andrew M. Greeley. *The Jesus Myth.* Garden City, N.Y.: Image Books, 1973.

Robert J. Karris. *Following Jesus: A Guide to the Gospels.* Chicago: Franciscan Herald Press, 1973.

Xavier Léon-Dufour. *Resurrection and the Message of Easter.* New York: Holt, Rinehart and Winston, 1974.

James M. Reese. *Preaching God's Burning Word.* Collegeville, Minn.: Liturgical Press, 1975.

Donald Senior. *Jesus: A Gospel Portrait.* Dayton, Ohio: Pflaum, 1975.